Pre-Algebra Practice

By

DR. BARBARA SANDALL, Ed.D.,
DR. MELFRIED OLSON, Ed.D.,
and TRAVIS OLSON, M.S.

COPYRIGHT © 2006 Mark Twain Media, Inc.

ISBN 10-digit: 1-58037-324-0
        13-digit: 978-1-58037-324-1

Printing No. CD-404041

Mark Twain Media, Inc., Publishers
Distributed by Carson-Dellosa Publishing LLC

Visit us at www.carsondellosa.com

This product has been correlated to state, national, and Canadian provincial standards. Visit www.carsondellosa.com to search and view its correlations to your standards.

Table of Contents

Table of Contents (cont.)

Introduction to the Math Practice Series

The *Math Practice series* will introduce students in middle school and high school to the course topics of Pre-Algebra, Algebra, Algebra II, and Geometry. The content of all of the practice books aligns with the Common Core State Standards for Mathematics. (© Copyright 2010. National Governors Association Center for Best Practices and Council of Chief State School Officers. All Rights Reserved.) The books are also aligned with the National Council of Teachers of Mathematics (NCTM) *Principles and Standards for School Mathematics*. (NCTM 2000)

This series is written for classroom teachers, parents, families, and students. The practice books in this series can be used as full units of study or as individual lessons to supplement textbooks or curriculum programs. Parents and students can use this series as an enhancement to what is being done in the classroom or as a tutorial at home. Students will be given a basic overview of the concepts, examples, practice problems, and challenge problems using the concepts introduced in the section. At the end of each section, there will be a set of problems to check progress on the concepts and a challenge set of problems over the whole section. At the end of the book, there will be check-up problems for each section that can be used for assessment.

According to the Mathematics Education Trust, new technologies require the fundamentals of algebra and algebraic thinking as a part of the background for all citizens. These technologies also provide opportunities to generate numerical examples, graph data, analyze patterns, and make generalizations. An understanding of algebra is also important because business and industry require higher levels of thinking and problem solving. Understanding geometry, including the characteristics and properties of two- and three-dimensional shapes, spatial relationships, symmetry, and the use of visualization and spatial reasoning, can also be used in solving problems.

While content and vocabulary are necessary, of equal importance are the processes of mathematics. Process skills include problem solving, reasoning, communication, and connections. The practice books in this series will address both the content and processes of algebra and algebraic thinking and geometry. This worktext, *Pre-Algebra Practice,* will help students transition from arithmetic to algebra.

Common Mathematics Symbols and Terms

Term	Symbol/Definition	Example
Addition sign	+	$2 + 2 = 4$
Subtraction sign	−	$4 − 2 = 2$
Multiplication sign	x or a dot • or 2 numbers or letters together or parentheses	3×2 $2 \cdot 2$ $2x$ $2(2)$
Division sign	÷ or a slash mark (/) or a horizontal fraction bar, or $\sqrt{}$	$6 \div 2$ $4/2$ $\frac{4}{2}$ $2\overline{)4}$
Equals or is equal to	=	$2 + 2 = 4$
Does Not Equal	≠	$5 \neq 1$
Parentheses – symbols for grouping numbers	( )	$(2 \times 5) + 3 =$
Pi – a number that is approximately $\frac{22}{7}$ or ≈ 3.14	π	$3.1415926\ldots$
Negative number – to the left of zero on a number line	−	-3
Positive number – to the right of zero on a number line	+	$+4$
Less than	<	$2 < 4$
Greater than	>	$4 > 2$
Greater than or equal to	≥	$2 + 3 \geq 4$
Less than or equal to	≤	$2 + 1 \leq 4$
Is approximately equal to	≈	$\pi \approx 3.14$
Radical sign	$\sqrt{}$	$\sqrt{9}$ The square root of 9 $\sqrt[3]{27}$ The cube root of 27
The _n_th power of _a_	a^n	$3^2 = 9$

Common Mathematics Symbols and Terms (cont.)

Variable	A letter used for an unknown number	$x + 8 = 12$ x is the letter representing the unknown number or variable
Mathematical Sentence	Contains two mathematical phrases joined by an equals (=) or an inequalities ($\neq$, $<$, $>$, $\leq$, $\geq$) sign	$2 + 3 = 5$ $9 - 3 > 5$ $3x + 8 = 20$
Equation	Mathematical sentence in which two phrases are connected with an equals (=) sign.	$5 + 7 = 12$ $3x = 12$ $1 = 1$
Mathematical Operations	Mathematics has four basic operations: addition, subtraction, multiplication, and division. Symbols are used for each operation.	+ sign indicates addition – sign indicates subtraction $\div$ indicates division • or x indicates multiplication
Like Terms	Can be all numbers or variables that are the same letter and same exponent	3, 4, 5 $3c$, $-5c$, $\frac{1}{2}c$ the variable is the same with the same exponent; they are like terms
Unlike Terms	Can be numbers or variables that are different	$5 + a$ Cannot be added because they are unlike terms $3x + 4y + 1z$ cannot be added because the variables are different, so they are unlike terms
Coefficient	The number in front of the variable (letter for the unknown number)	$5x$ In this number, 5 is the coefficient.
Identity Property of Addition	Any number or variable added to zero is that number or variable.	$0 + 5 = 5$ $-3 + 0 = -3$ $a + 0 = a$
Identity Property of Multiplication	Any number or variable times 1 is equal to that number or variable.	$12 • 1 = 12$ $b • 1 = b$ $3y • 1 = 3y$

Common Mathematics Symbols and Terms (cont.)

Commutative Property of Addition	No matter the order in which you add two numbers, the sum is always the same.	$4 + 7 = 7 + 4$ $b + c = c + b$
Commutative Property of Multiplication	No matter the order in which you multiply two numbers, the answer is always the same.	$20 \times \frac{1}{2} = \frac{1}{2} \times 20$ $5 \cdot 3 = 3 \cdot 5$ $a \cdot b = b \cdot a$
Associative Property of Addition	No matter the order in which you add three numbers together, the the sum will always be the same.	$(5 + 6) + 7 = 5 + (6 + 7)$ $(a + b) + c = a + (b + c)$
Associative Property of Multiplication	No matter the order in which you group numbers when you multiply, the answer will always be the same product.	$(5 \cdot 4) \cdot 8 = 5 \cdot (4 \cdot 8)$ $(a \cdot b) \cdot c = a \cdot (b \cdot c)$
Distributive Property of Multiplication Over Addition	Allows the choice of multiplication followed by addition or addition followed by multiplication.	$3(5 + 2) = 3 \cdot 5 + 3 \cdot 2$ $a(b + c) = a \cdot b + a \cdot c$
Inverse Operation	Operation that cancels another operation	Multiplication and division $5 \cdot x = 5x$ $\frac{5x}{5} = x$ Addition and Subtraction $n + 5 - 5 = n$
Reciprocal or Multiplicative Inverse Property	Two numbers are multiplied, and the product is 1.	For any non-zero number: Number $\times \dfrac{1}{\text{Number}} = 1$ $\dfrac{1}{\text{Number}} \times$ Number $= 1$ $a \cdot \dfrac{1}{a} = 1$ $5 \cdot \dfrac{1}{5} = 1$

Common Mathematics Symbols and Terms (cont.)

Exponents	Shorthand for repeated multiplication	$a^2 = a \cdot a$ $y^4 = y \cdot y \cdot y \cdot y$
Square Numbers	The result of multiplying a number or variable by itself	$4 \cdot 4 = 16$ $a \cdot a = a^2$
Square Roots	A square root indicated by the radical sign $\sqrt{}$ is the number multiplied by itself to get the radicand.	$\sqrt{9}$ What number multiplied by itself = 9? $3 \cdot 3 = 9$ So $\sqrt{9} = 3$
Radicand	Number under the radical	$\sqrt{9}$ 9 is the radicand
Numerator	Top number in a fraction	$\frac{3}{5}$ In this fraction, 3 is the numerator
Denominator	Bottom number in a fraction	$\frac{3}{5}$ In this fraction, 5 is the denominator
Integers	Natural numbers, their opposites, or negative numbers, and zero	Set of Integers: $\{...-3,-2,-1,0,1,2,3...\}$
Additive Inverse Property of Addition	The sum of an integer and its opposite integer will always be zero.	$a + -a = 0$ $5 + -5 = 0$
Set	Specific group of numbers or objects	Set of Integers: $\{...-3,-2,-1,0,1,2,3...\}$
Absolute Value	|a| The absolute value of a number can be considered as the distance between the number and zero on a number line. The absolute value of every number will be either positive or zero. Real numbers come in pared opposites, *a* and -*a*, that are the same distance from the origin, but in opposite directions. ← + + + + + + + + → -3 -2 -1 0 1 2 3	Absolute value of *a* |a| = a |-a| = a If *a* is 0, |a| = 0. If 0 is the origin on the number line on the left, 3 is the absolute value of the pair -3 and +3 because they are both 3 marks from 0.

Name: _____ Date: _____

Chapter 1: Real Numbers

Basic Overview: Real Numbers

All types of numbers are needed in working to solve problems. Algebra uses numbers, symbols, and letters to solve problems. Types of numbers described in this section include real, rational, irrational, integers, whole, and natural.

Examples of Real Numbers:

Real numbers are a combination of all the number systems listed below.

Rational numbers can be expressed as the ratio of two integers (denominator not equal to zero), and when expressed in decimal form, they either repeat or terminate.

$$\frac{3}{1} \qquad \frac{1}{4} \qquad \frac{2}{3} \qquad 0.35$$

Irrational numbers cannot be expressed as a ratio of two integers, and when expressed in decimal form, they neither repeat nor terminate.

$$\sqrt{2} \qquad \sqrt{3}$$

π is the symbol for pi. The decimal form of pi is 3.14 ....

0.010110111101111.... and it continues. This pattern never ends, and it does not repeat.

Integers include natural numbers, their opposites or negative numbers, and zero:

-5   0   3   17,777

Whole numbers are the natural numbers plus zero:

0   33   1,289   2

Natural numbers are sometimes called counting numbers:

3   1,777   5   1

Name: _____   Date: _____

Chapter 1: Real Numbers (cont.)

Practice: Which Number Is Which?

Directions: Using the words listed below, fill in the blanks with the correct number type(s).

Real Number	Rational Number	Integer	Whole Number	Irrational Number

	Number	Type or Types
1.	5	1, 2, 3, 4
2.	-3	1, 2, 3,
3.	0.12	2, 1
4.	0.12121212 …	2, 1
5.	0.12123123412345	1, 5
6.	$\sqrt{49}$	1, 2, 3, 4
7.	-4.23	2, 1
8.	$\frac{52}{13}$	2, 1,
9.	$1.\overline{212}$	1, 2,
10.	π^2	1, 5
11.	12 ÷ 15	1, 3, 4, 2
12.	$\sqrt{13}$	1, 5,
13.	-999999	1, 3, 4, 5
14.	23,323,332,333,323,333,333	1, 3, 4, 2
15.	$\frac{5.2}{13}$	1, 2
16.	$\sqrt{\sqrt{49}}$	1, 2
17.	-5,300,000	1, 5, 3,
18.	$\frac{13}{65}$	1, 2
19.	3.2 + 4.8	1, 5, 3
20.	x	1, 5,

Name: _____   Date: _____

Chapter 1: Real Numbers (cont.)

Challenge Problems: Real Numbers

Directions: Using the words listed below, fill in the blanks with the correct number type(s).

Real Number	Rational Number	Integer	Whole Number	Irrational Number

Number   **Type or Types**

1. -0   3 | 2

2. $4 \div \sqrt{4}$ 1 2 3 4

3. $-\sqrt{\frac{48}{3}}$ 1 3,2

4. $\sqrt{-4}$ 13 None

5. 0.999999999999999…   5 | 2

6. $\sqrt[3]{\frac{8}{2}}$ 1 3 4

7. 0.0000000000000000000001   1 2

8. $\frac{2\pi}{5\pi}$ 5 1

9. $1 - 2 + 3 - 4 + 5$ 1 2 3 4

10. $4 \cdot 3.5$ 1 2 3 4

Name: _____ Date: _____

Chapter 1: Real Numbers (cont.)

Checking Progress: Real Numbers

Directions: Using the words listed below, fill in the blanks with the correct number type(s).

Real Number	Rational Number	Integer	Whole Number	Irrational Number

Number		**Type or Types**
1.	-3.2	1, 2
2.	$\sqrt{50}$	1, 5
3.	$\sqrt{121}$	1, 2, 3, 4
4.	$\frac{23}{47}$	1, 2
5.	π	1, 5
6.	0.134134134 …	1, 2
7.	0.134	1, 2
8.	13^2	1, 2, 3, 4
9.	134,134,134,134	1, 2, 3, 4
10.	$\frac{\pi}{4}$	1, 5

Name: _____ Date: _____

Chapter 2: Operations of Numbers and Variables

Basic Overview: Addition and Subtraction

When doing addition, only add like terms. A **like term** is any number or variable that uses the same letter as another. When you add variables that are the same, you add the **coefficients**, or the numbers in front of the variable. Only like terms can be subtracted. One number can be subtracted from another and one variable (an unknown number represented by a letter) can be subtracted from another if they are the same variable.

Examples of Addition and Subtraction:

3 bottles of sports drink + 7 bottles of sports drink = 10 bottles of sports drink

5 protein bars – 2 protein bars eaten = 3 protein bars left

$2b + 0 = 2b$

$4 - 0 = 4$

Practice: Addition and Subtraction of Numbers and Variables

Directions: Perform the following operations. If you cannot perform the operation, explain why the operation cannot be done. Whenever possible, try these mentally and use pencil and paper or a calculator only as needed. Look for underlying ideas being presented rather than only thinking of these practice problems as a computation to perform.

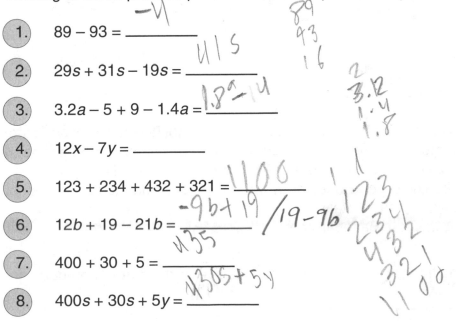

1. $89 - 93 =$ _____

2. $29s + 31s - 19s =$ _____

3. $3.2a - 5 + 9 - 1.4a =$ _____

4. $12x - 7y =$ _____

5. $123 + 234 + 432 + 321 =$ _____

6. $12b + 19 - 21b =$ _____

7. $400 + 30 + 5 =$ _____

8. $400s + 30s + 5y =$ _____

Chapter 2: Operations of Numbers and Variables (cont.)

9. $-400s + 30s + 5s =$ _~~-3.65 5~~_

10. $-400s + -30s + -5s =$ _-435 s_

11. $-400s - 30s - 5s =$ _-435s_

12. $3{,}245 - 200 - 40 - 5 =$ _3000_

13. $87 + 92 - 87 + 92 =$ _184_

14. $87 + 92 - 87 - 92 =$ _0_

15. $87x + 92y - 87y - 92x =$ _-5x+5y_

16. $3{,}000 + 300 + 30 + 3 - 2{,}000 - 200 - 20 - 2 =$ _||||_

17. $3{,}000a + 300a + 30a + 3a - 2{,}000b - 200b - 20b - 2b =$ _3333a - 2222b_

18. $2.3 + 4.23 + 7.423 =$ _13.953_

19. $\frac{1}{2} + \frac{1}{3} =$ _5/6_

20. $\frac{1}{2}s + \frac{1}{3} =$ _~~5/6 s~~_ *Cannot be continued*

Challenge Problems: Addition and Subtraction of Numbers and Variables

1. $a + b + c + 2a + 2b + 2c - 3a - 3b - 3c =$ _0_

2. $46 - 9z - 46 =$ _-9z_

3. $x + 2y + 3z + 4w + 5a + 6b =$ _Cannot be continued_

4. Jamal was an avid baseball card collector. For the summer, he got his dream job working in Mr. Garcia's sports memorabilia shop. Mr. Garcia agreed to pay Jamal $7.50 per hour in wages and one new baseball card for every five hours he works. During the first week, he worked 30 hours; the second week he worked 20 hours; and the third week he worked 25 hours. What was Jamal's total wages, and how many baseball cards did he earn?   Wages _35.25_   Baseball cards _15_

5. Write a problem with addition and subtraction that uses five terms that will produce an answer of $5b - 29$. _20b÷4-[32-3-29]x8+29_

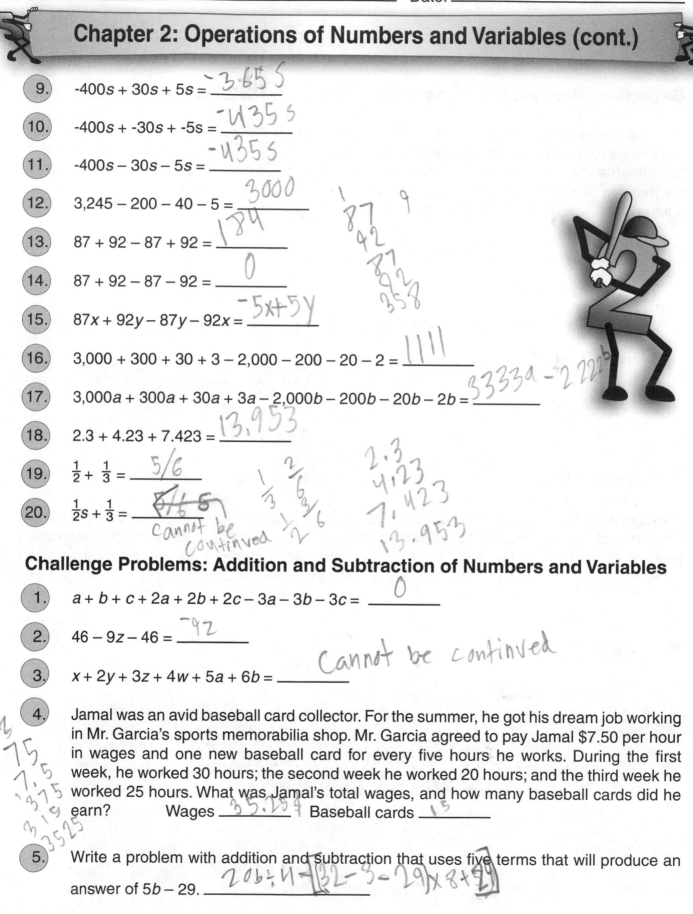

Name: _____ Date: _____

Chapter 2: Operations of Numbers and Variables (cont.)

Basic Overview: Multiplication of Numbers and Variables

Any like or unlike terms can be multiplied. Numbers or variables (letters representing an unknown number) can be multiplied. A number times a variable or coefficient can be multiplied.

Examples of Multiplying Numbers and Variables:

$22 \cdot 5 = 110$

$a \cdot b = ab$

$5 \cdot a = 5a$

$5a \cdot 4c = 20ac$

$2a \cdot 0 = 0$

Practice: Multiplication of Numbers and Variables

Directions: Perform the following operations. If you cannot perform the operation, explain why the operation cannot be done. Whenever possible, try these mentally, and use pencil and paper or a calculator only as needed. Look for underlying ideas being presented rather than only thinking of these practice problems as a computation to perform.

1. $\frac{1}{3} \cdot \frac{2}{3} =$ _____

2. $\frac{5}{6} \cdot \frac{4}{5} \cdot \frac{3}{4} \cdot \frac{2}{3} \cdot \frac{1}{2} =$ _____

3. $3a \cdot 5b =$ _____

4. $48 \cdot 12 =$ _____

5. $43.2345 \cdot 0.01 =$ _____

6. $43.2345a \cdot 0.1b =$ _____

7. $39s \cdot 0.25t =$ _____

8. $\frac{5}{6}a \cdot 36b \cdot \frac{2}{3}c =$ _____

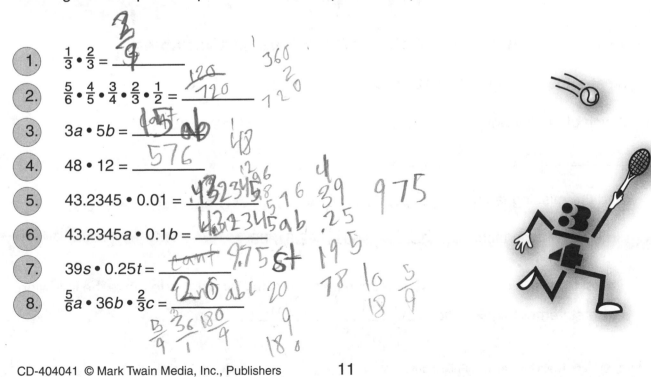

Chapter 2: Operations of Numbers and Variables (cont.)

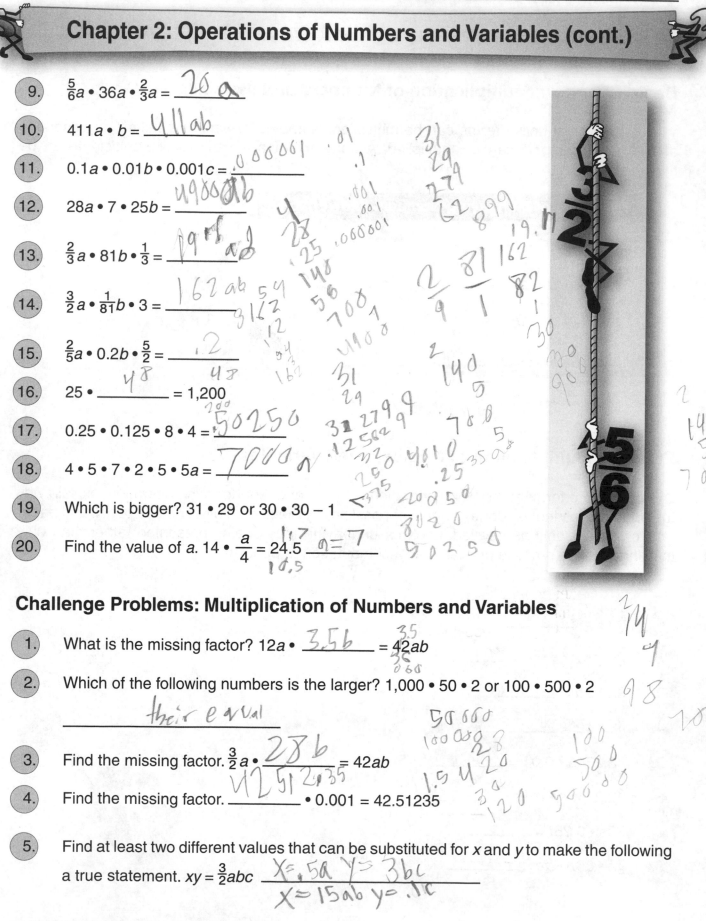

9. $\frac{5}{6}a \cdot 36a \cdot \frac{2}{3}a =$ __20a__

10. $411a \cdot b =$ __411ab__

11. $0.1a \cdot 0.01b \cdot 0.001c =$ __.000001__

12. $28a \cdot 7 \cdot 25b =$ __4900ab__

13. $\frac{2}{3}a \cdot 81b \cdot \frac{1}{3} =$ __18 a__

14. $\frac{3}{2}a \cdot \frac{1}{81}b \cdot 3 =$ __162 ab__

15. $\frac{2}{5}a \cdot 0.2b \cdot \frac{5}{2} =$ __.2__

16. $25 \cdot$ __48__ $= 1,200$

17. $0.25 \cdot 0.125 \cdot 8 \cdot 4 =$ __50250__

18. $4 \cdot 5 \cdot 7 \cdot 2 \cdot 5 \cdot 5a =$ __7000__

19. Which is bigger? $31 \cdot 29$ or $30 \cdot 30 - 1$ _____

20. Find the value of a. $14 \cdot \frac{a}{4} = 24.5$ __a = 7__

Challenge Problems: Multiplication of Numbers and Variables

1. What is the missing factor? $12a \cdot$ __3.5b__ $= 42ab$

2. Which of the following numbers is the larger? $1,000 \cdot 50 \cdot 2$ or $100 \cdot 500 \cdot 2$
    __their equal__

3. Find the missing factor. $\frac{3}{2}a \cdot$ __28b__ $= 42ab$

4. Find the missing factor. _____ $\cdot 0.001 = 42.51235$

5. Find at least two different values that can be substituted for x and y to make the following
    a true statement. $xy = \frac{3}{2}abc$ __X = .5a Y = 3bc__
    __X = 15ab y = .1c__

Name: _____   Date: _____

Chapter 2: Operations of Numbers and Variables (cont.)

Basic Overview: Division of Numbers and Variables

Like and unlike terms can be divided and so can any two numbers or variables. Phrases with numbers and variables can also be divided. When adding or subtracting zero and any number or variable, the answer is the number or variable.

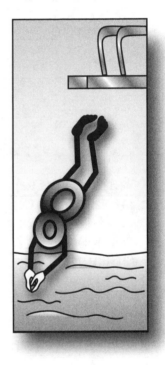

Examples of Dividing Numbers and Variables:

$8 \div 4 = 2$

$a \div b = \dfrac{a}{b}$

$6a \div 2a = 3$

$12c \div 3d = 4\dfrac{c}{d}$

$0 \div (-6) = 0$

$4 \div 0 =$ cannot be divided.

$a \div 0 =$ cannot be divided.

Practice: Division of Numbers and Variables

Directions: Perform the following operations. If you cannot perform the operation, explain why the operation cannot be done. Whenever possible, try these mentally, and use pencil and paper or a calculator only as needed. Look for underlying ideas being presented rather than only thinking of these practice problems as a computation to perform. When a variable is used in the denominator, assume that the value is not zero.

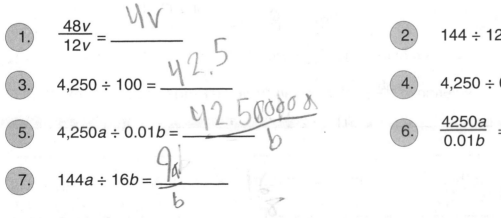

1. $\dfrac{48v}{12v} =$ _____ 4v

2. $144 \div 12 =$ _____ 12

3. $4{,}250 \div 100 =$ _____ 42.5

4. $4{,}250 \div 0.01 =$ _____ 425000

5. $4{,}250a \div 0.01b =$ _____ $\dfrac{42.500000}{b}$

6. $\dfrac{4250a}{0.01b} =$ _____ $\dfrac{42.500}{b}$

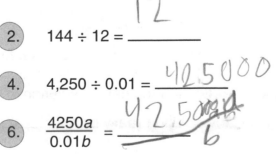

7. $144a \div 16b =$ _____ $\dfrac{9a}{b}$

Name: _____   Date: _____

Chapter 2: Operations of Numbers and Variables (cont.)

8. What is the value of a? $a \cdot \frac{1}{3} = \frac{3}{5}$ _____

9. Which is larger? $42 \div 0.234$ or $420 \div 2.34$ _____

10. Which is larger? $42a \div 0.234b$ or $420a \div 2.34b$ _____

11. $0 \div 291 =$ _____

12. $\frac{56yz}{12xz} =$ _____

13. $212xyz \div$ _____ $= 424y$

14. _____ $\div 12xyz = 12y$

15. $\frac{(32yz)(4z)(5yz)}{(16xz)(10yz)(12z)} =$ _____

16. $\frac{(32)(4)(5)}{(16)(10)(12)} =$ _____

17. $\frac{88}{11} - \frac{48}{6} =$ _____

18. Which of these has the larger value? $\frac{12}{37} \div \frac{4}{31}$ or $\frac{12}{37} \cdot \frac{31}{4}$ _____

19. Which of these has the larger value? $\frac{12}{37} \div \frac{4}{31}$ or $\frac{31}{12} \cdot \frac{4}{31}$ _____

20. $0.02324 \div$ _____ $= 23.24$

Challenge Problems: Dividing Numbers and Variables

1. $\frac{142}{317} \div \frac{2}{317} =$ _____

2. $\frac{142}{317} \div 0 =$ _____

3. Find two solutions for a and b to the following problem. $a \div b = \frac{25xy}{6x}$ _____

4. Brad thought that the solution to $\frac{88-48}{11-6}$ was 0. Why would Brad think this? What should the solution really be? _____

_____

5. Stewart thought that these two expressions were the same. $\frac{1}{3}a$ and $\frac{a}{3}$. What do you think? _____

Name: _____   Date: _____

Chapter 2: Operations of Numbers and Variables (cont.)

Basic Overview: Order of Operations

When solving mathematical expressions that have more than one operation, it is important to do the operations in the correct order.

1. Do the operations within parentheses first; If the parentheses are nested, work outward from the innermost parentheses.
2. Find the value of any number with an exponent.
3. Multiple and/or divide, working from left to right.
4. Add and/or subtract, working from left to right.

Examples of Order of Operations:

1. Do the operations in the parentheses; if there are no parentheses, do the operations from left to right.
    $8(25 - 5) =$ _160_
    Do the operation in the parentheses first. $(25 - 5) = 20$
    So the problem is $8(20) =$
    Then multiply. $8(20) = 160$

2. Find the value of any number with an exponent.
    $5 \cdot 4^2 =$
    Find the value of the number with the exponent. $4^2 = 16$
    Then multiply. $5 \cdot 16 = 80$
    $5 \cdot 4^2 = 80$

3. Multiply or divide first, then add.
    $8 \cdot 5 + 4 \cdot 5 =$
    If there are no parentheses, do the operations from left to right.
    Do the multiplication first. $8 \cdot 5 = 40; 4 \cdot 5 = 20$
    Then do the addition. $40 + 20 = 60$
    $8 \cdot 5 + 4 \cdot 5 = 60$

4. Multiply or divide first, then add or subtract.
    $6 \cdot 5 - 4 \cdot 5 =$
    If there are no parentheses, do the operations from left to right.
    Do the multiplication first. $6 \cdot 5 = 30; 4 \cdot 5 = 20$
    Then do the subtraction. $30 - 20 = 10$
    $6 \cdot 5 - 4 \cdot 5 = 10$

Name: _____ Date: _____

Chapter 2: Operations of Numbers and Variables (cont.)

Practice: Order of Operations

Directions: Solve the following problems, using the correct order of operations. When a variable is used in the denominator, assume that the value is not zero.

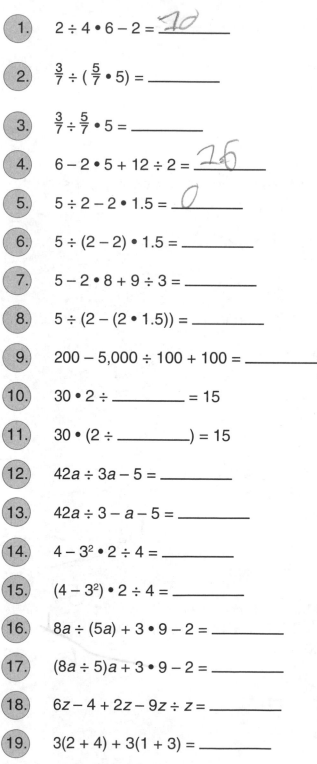

1. $2 \div 4 \cdot 6 - 2 =$ _~~10~~_

2. $\frac{3}{7} \div (\frac{5}{7} \cdot 5) =$ _____

3. $\frac{3}{7} \div \frac{5}{7} \cdot 5 =$ _____

4. $6 - 2 \cdot 5 + 12 \div 2 =$ _~~26~~_

5. $5 \div 2 - 2 \cdot 1.5 =$ _0_

6. $5 \div (2 - 2) \cdot 1.5 =$ _____

7. $5 - 2 \cdot 8 + 9 \div 3 =$ _____

8. $5 \div (2 - (2 \cdot 1.5)) =$ _____

9. $200 - 5{,}000 \div 100 + 100 =$ _____

10. $30 \cdot 2 \div$ _____ $= 15$

11. $30 \cdot (2 \div$ _____ $) = 15$

12. $42a \div 3a - 5 =$ _____

13. $42a \div 3 - a - 5 =$ _____

14. $4 - 3^2 \cdot 2 \div 4 =$ _____

15. $(4 - 3^2) \cdot 2 \div 4 =$ _____

16. $8a \div (5a) + 3 \cdot 9 - 2 =$ _____

17. $(8a \div 5)a + 3 \cdot 9 - 2 =$ _____

18. $6z - 4 + 2z - 9z \div z =$ _____

19. $3(2 + 4) + 3(1 + 3) =$ _____

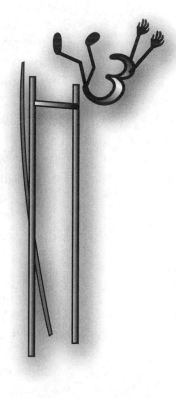

16

Name: _____   Date: _____

Chapter 2: Operations of Numbers and Variables (cont.)

20. $2 - 3^2(4 - 5) =$ _____

21. $32 \div 8 \div 2 \cdot 8 \cdot 2 =$ _____

22. $81^5 \cdot (49 - 7^2) =$ _____

23. $16 \cdot 5 - 12 \cdot 5 - 4 \cdot 5 =$ _____

24. $\frac{180}{55} \cdot 11 \cdot 5 =$ _____

25. $11 \cdot 180 \div 55 \cdot 5 =$ _____

26. $54 \div 7 - 28 \div 7 - 25 \div 7 =$ _____

27. $82a - 28a +$ _____ $= 100a$

28. $\frac{2}{a} + \frac{4}{a} + \frac{122}{a} =$ _____

29. $128a + 12a -$ _____ $= 72a$

30. $\frac{12}{4^2 - 2^4} =$ _____

31. $12 \cdot 4^2 - 2^4 - 10 \cdot 16 =$ _____

32. $6^2 + (3^3 - 8) - 5 =$ _____

33. $92 - 8 \cdot 9 - 5 \cdot 8 =$ _____

34. $(92 - 8) \cdot (9 - 5 \cdot 8) =$ _____

35. $(92 - 8 \cdot 9 - 5) \cdot 8 =$ _____

36. $9(2 - 8 \cdot 9 - 5 \cdot 8) =$ _____

37. $9(2 - 8) \cdot (9 - 5) \cdot 8 =$ _____

38. $53(9^2 - 5 -$ _____ $) = 0$

39. $\dfrac{32 + 5 - \rule{1.5cm}{0.4pt}}{543^3} = 0$

40. $9s + 3(8 - s) + 13 + 3s =$ _____

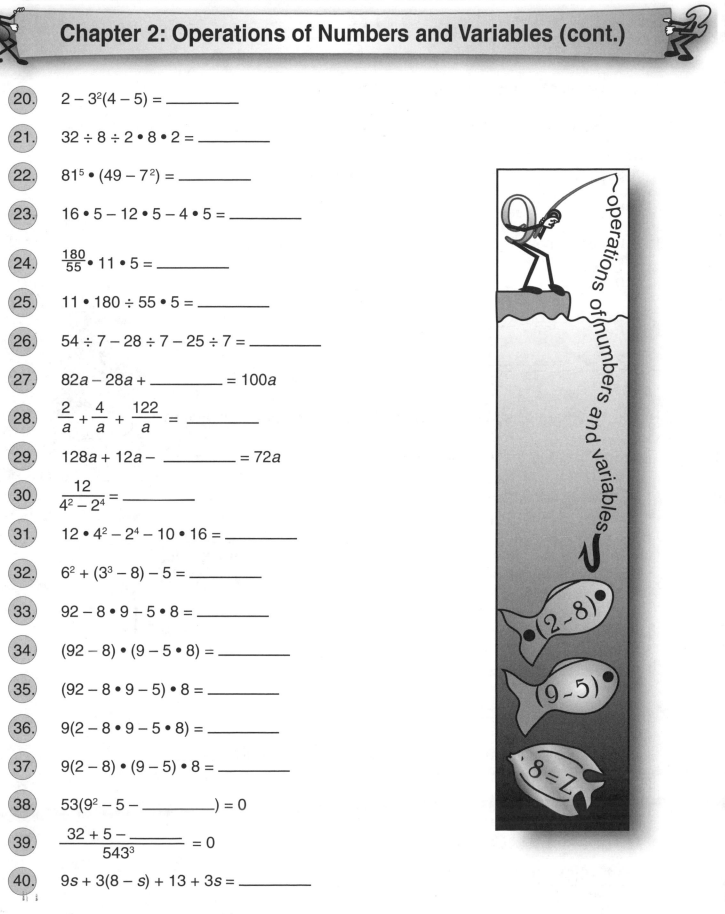

Name: _____ Date: _____

Chapter 2: Operations of Numbers and Variables (cont.)

Challenge Problems: Order of Operations

1. Place parentheses into the expression to make a true statement. $2 \cdot 5 - 3 + 8 = 12$

2. Place values in the expression to make a true statement.

   (_____ − _____) • _____ ÷ (_____ + _____) = 20

3. Which of these expressions is the larger? -4^2 or $(-4)^2$ _____

4. $(3 \cdot 2 - 5 \cdot 4 + (2 - 9)) \cdot 0 + 32 \div 4 - 2 =$ _____

5. $5^{(8 - 2 \cdot 3)} - \dfrac{9}{3^2} =$ _____

6. $2^a + 3^a =$ _____

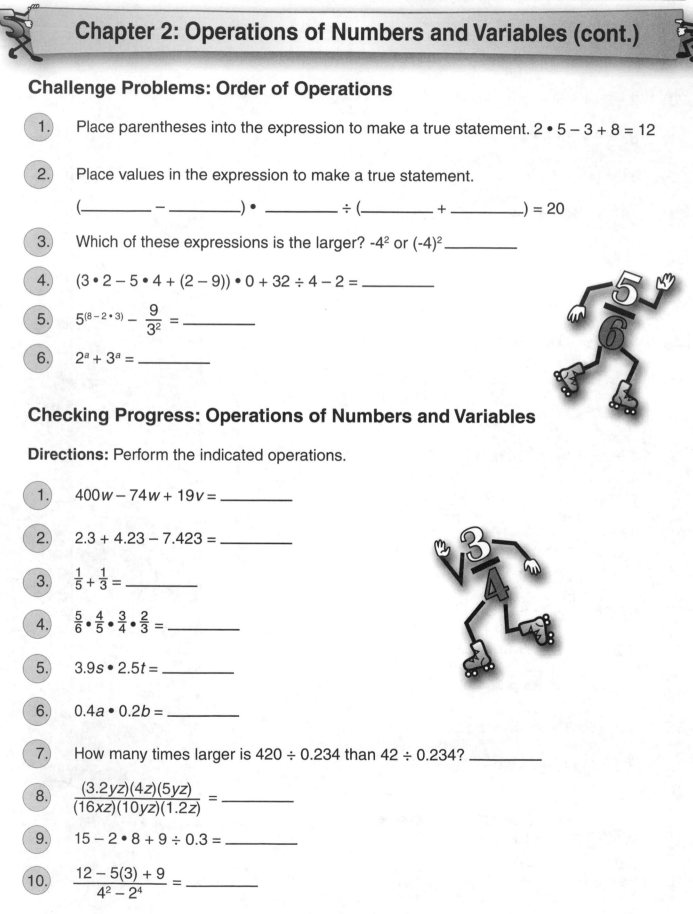

Checking Progress: Operations of Numbers and Variables

Directions: Perform the indicated operations.

1. $400w - 74w + 19v =$ _____

2. $2.3 + 4.23 - 7.423 =$ _____

3. $\dfrac{1}{5} + \dfrac{1}{3} =$ _____

4. $\dfrac{5}{6} \cdot \dfrac{4}{5} \cdot \dfrac{3}{4} \cdot \dfrac{2}{3} =$ _____

5. $3.9s \cdot 2.5t =$ _____

6. $0.4a \cdot 0.2b =$ _____

7. How many times larger is $420 \div 0.234$ than $42 \div 0.234$? _____

8. $\dfrac{(3.2yz)(4z)(5yz)}{(16xz)(10yz)(1.2z)} =$ _____

9. $15 - 2 \cdot 8 + 9 \div 0.3 =$ _____

10. $\dfrac{12 - 5(3) + 9}{4^2 - 2^4} =$ _____

Name: _____ Date: _____

Chapter 3: Integers

Basic Overview: Positive and Negative Integers

The number line for whole numbers starts at zero and uses equally spaced marks to represent 1, 2, 3 and the other numbers that belong to the infinite set of whole numbers.

Whole Number Line

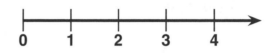

The set of whole numbers and negative numbers is called the **integers**. These can be defined as **the set of integers** {…,-3, -2, -1, 0, 1, 2, 3, …} and can be illustrated by using a number line.

Integer Number Line

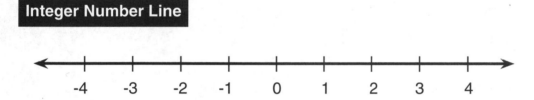

Basic Overview: Addition and Subtraction of Integers

For every integer, a, there is a unique integer, $-a$ so that, $a + (-a) = 0$. The integer $-a$ is called the **additive inverse** of a.

When subtracting integers, connect what is known about the subtraction of whole numbers and basic subtraction facts.

Example of Additive Inverse:

$-5 + 5 = 0$

Examples of Adding Two Integers:

$-34 + 52 = 18$ $25 + 12 = 27$

Examples of Subtracting Integers:

$35 - 47 = -8$ $-8 - 4 = -12$

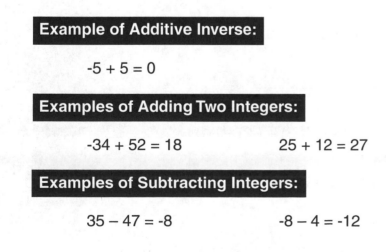

Name: _____   Date: _____

Chapter 3: Integers (cont.)

Practice: Addition and Subtraction of Integers

Directions: Perform the indicated operations.

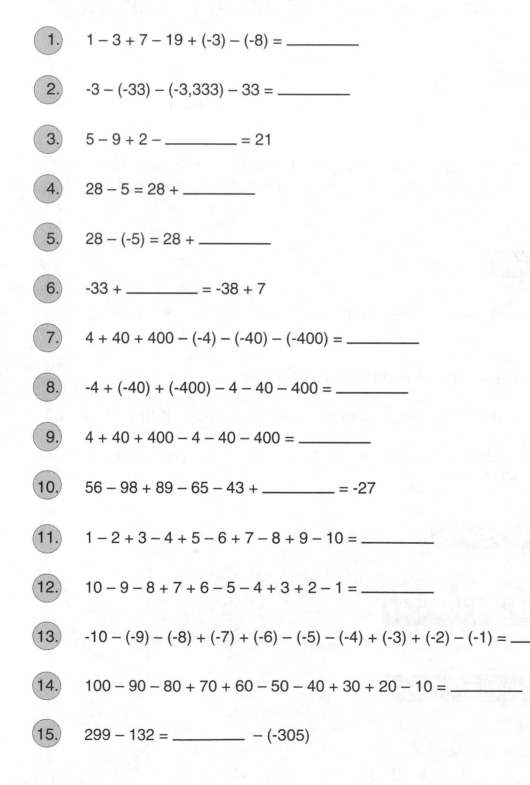

1. $1 - 3 + 7 - 19 + (-3) - (-8) =$ _____

2. $-3 - (-33) - (-3{,}333) - 33 =$ _____

3. $5 - 9 + 2 -$ _____ $= 21$

4. $28 - 5 = 28 +$ _____

5. $28 - (-5) = 28 +$ _____

6. $-33 +$ _____ $= -38 + 7$

7. $4 + 40 + 400 - (-4) - (-40) - (-400) =$ _____

8. $-4 + (-40) + (-400) - 4 - 40 - 400 =$ _____

9. $4 + 40 + 400 - 4 - 40 - 400 =$ _____

10. $56 - 98 + 89 - 65 - 43 +$ _____ $= -27$

11. $1 - 2 + 3 - 4 + 5 - 6 + 7 - 8 + 9 - 10 =$ _____

12. $10 - 9 - 8 + 7 + 6 - 5 - 4 + 3 + 2 - 1 =$ _____

13. $-10 - (-9) - (-8) + (-7) + (-6) - (-5) - (-4) + (-3) + (-2) - (-1) =$ _____

14. $100 - 90 - 80 + 70 + 60 - 50 - 40 + 30 + 20 - 10 =$ _____

15. $299 - 132 =$ _____ $- (-305)$

Name: _____ Date: _____

Chapter 3: Integers (cont.)

16. _____ + (-305) = 489,341 − 305

17. 3,213 + (-3,605) = _____

18. 3,213 − (-3,605) = _____

19. -3,213 − (-3,605) = _____

20. 293 − 312 − 102 + 212 − _____ = 1,000

Challenge Problems: Addition and Subtraction of Integers

1. What are five pairs of integers with both integers less than zero that will satisfy the following equation? $a - b = 7$ _____

2. Which number is larger? 43,526 − 29,098,090 or 43,526 − (-29,098,090) _____

3. 3 − 4 − 5 − 6 − 7 − 8 = 28 − _____ − 4 − 5 − 6 − 7 − 8

4. 10 − (-9) − (-8) − (-7) − (-6) − (-5) − (-4) − (-3) − (-2) − (-1) = _____

5. 100 − (-90) − (-80) − (-70) − (-60) − (-50) − (-40) − (-30) − (-20) − (-10) = _____

6. |9 + 2 − 9 − 4| − |-9 + 2 − 9 − 4| = _____

Name: _____ Date: _____

Chapter 3: Integers (cont.)

Basic Overview: Multiplication and Division of Integers

The multiplication of integers uses what you already know about the multiplication of whole numbers. Multiplying two positive integers results in a positive integer answer. Multiply a positive and a negative integer as if both were positive, and make the final answer negative. Multiply two negative integers as if both were positive, and make the final answer positive. Learning division is simply a matter of connecting division to multiplication. Since division and multiplication are inverse operations, integer division is built on what we already know.

Examples of Multiplying Integers:

$3 \cdot 5 = 15$

$3 \cdot -5 = -15$

Examples of Dividing Integers:

$15 \div 3 = 5$

$-15 \div 3 = -5$

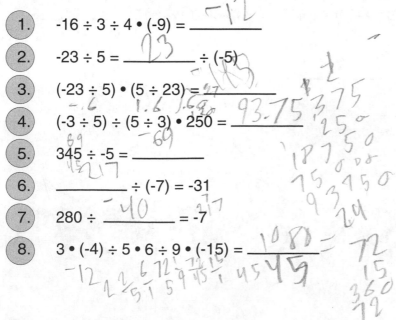

Practice: Multiplication and Division of Integers

Directions: Perform the indicated operations.

1. $-16 \div 3 \div 4 \cdot (-9) = $ _____

2. $-23 \div 5 = $ _____ $\div (-5)$

3. $(-23 \div 5) \cdot (5 \div 23) = $ _____

4. $(-3 \div 5) \div (5 \div 3) \cdot 250 = $ _____

5. $345 \div -5 = $ _____

6. _____ $\div (-7) = -31$

7. $280 \div $ _____ $= -7$

8. $3 \cdot (-4) \div 5 \cdot 6 \div 9 \cdot (-15) = $ _____

Name: _____ Date: _____

Chapter 3: Integers (cont.)

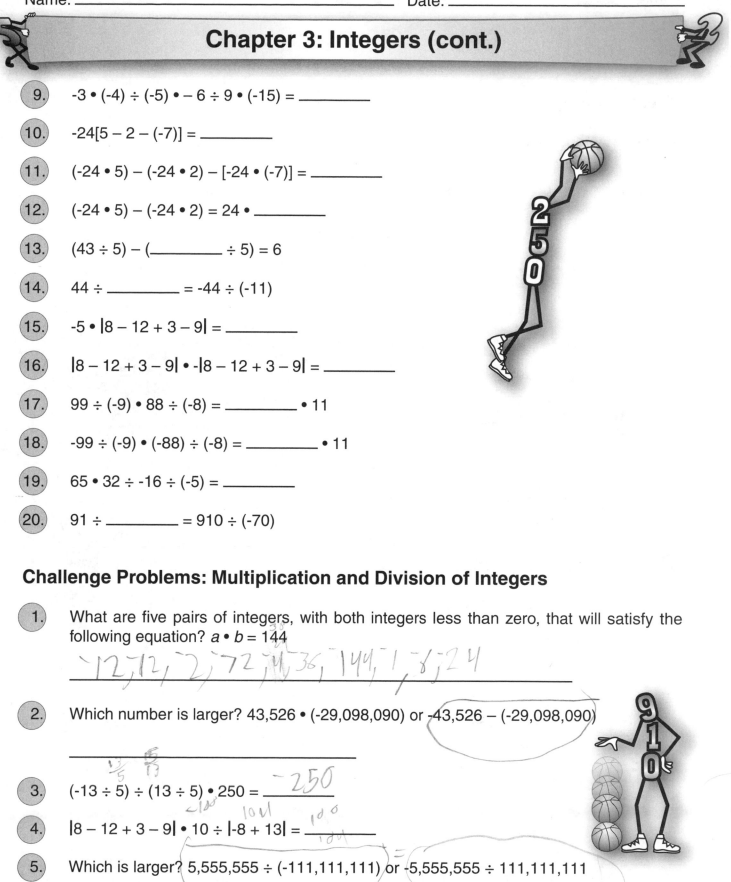

9. -3 • (-4) ÷ (-5) • − 6 ÷ 9 • (-15) = _____

10. -24[5 − 2 − (-7)] = _____

11. (-24 • 5) − (-24 • 2) − [-24 • (-7)] = _____

12. (-24 • 5) − (-24 • 2) = 24 • _____

13. (43 ÷ 5) − (_____ ÷ 5) = 6

14. 44 ÷ _____ = -44 ÷ (-11)

15. -5 • |8 − 12 + 3 − 9| = _____

16. |8 − 12 + 3 − 9| • -|8 − 12 + 3 − 9| = _____

17. 99 ÷ (-9) • 88 ÷ (-8) = _____ • 11

18. -99 ÷ (-9) • (-88) ÷ (-8) = _____ • 11

19. 65 • 32 ÷ -16 ÷ (-5) = _____

20. 91 ÷ _____ = 910 ÷ (-70)

Challenge Problems: Multiplication and Division of Integers

1. What are five pairs of integers, with both integers less than zero, that will satisfy the following equation? $a • b = 144$

    ‾12, 12, ‾2, 72, ‾4, 36, ‾144, 1, ‾8, 24

2. Which number is larger? 43,526 • (-29,098,090) or -43,526 − (-29,098,090)

    13/5 6/13

3. (-13 ÷ 5) ÷ (13 ÷ 5) • 250 = __-250__

4. |8 − 12 + 3 − 9| • 10 ÷ |-8 + 13| = __100__

5. Which is larger? 5,555,555 ÷ (-111,111,111) or -5,555,555 ÷ 111,111,111

_____

Name: _____ Date: _____

Chapter 3: Integers (cont.)

Checking Progress: All Integers

Directions: Perform the indicated operations.

1. $10 - 9 - 18 + 7 + 6 - 5 + 14 + 3 - 2 - 1 =$ _____

2. $-10 + (-9) - (-8) - (-7) + (-6) - (-5) - (-4) =$ _____

3. $10 - 9 - 80 + 70 + 6 - 50 - 40 + 30 =$ _____

4. $299 - 1,132 =$ _____ $- (-305)$

5. _____ $- (-305) = 89,341 - 305$

6. $(-24 \cdot 5) + (-24 \cdot 2) - [-24 \cdot (-7)] =$ _____

7. $(-24 \cdot 5) - (24 \cdot 2) = 24 \cdot$ _____

8. $(43 \div 5) - ($ _____ $\div 5) = 10$

9. $-24 \cdot 5 = 24 \cdot$ _____

10. $-15 \cdot -|8 - 12 + 3 - 9| =$ _____

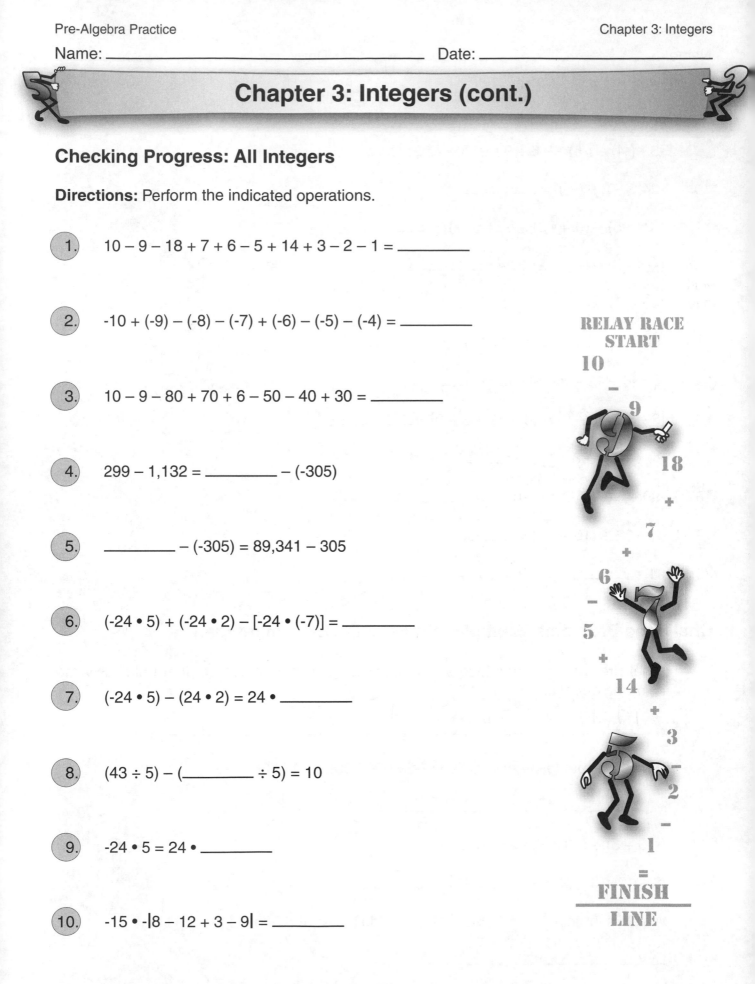

RELAY RACE
START
10
–
9
18
+
7
+
6
–
5
+
14
+
3
–
2
–
1
=
FINISH
LINE

Name: _____ Date: _____

Chapter 4: Properties

Basic Overview: Identity and Inverse Properties of Addition and Multiplication

Number operations have certain properties or rules. The properties related to algebra include the Identity Properties, Commutative Properties, and Associative Properties of Addition and Multiplication, and the Distributive Property of Multiplication Over Addition.

When adding or subtracting zero and any number or variable, the answer is the number or variable. This is the Identity Property of Addition and Subtraction. The Identity Property of Multiplication states that any number or variable multiplied by 1 is that number or variable. Inverse operations are operations that cancel each other. For example, addition and subtraction are inverse operations. Reciprocal or Multiplicative Inverse Operations are operations in which two numbers are multiplied, and the product is 1.

Examples of the Identity Property of Addition:

$4 + 0 = 4$

$a + 0 = a$

$2b + 0 = 2b$

Examples of the Identity Property of Multiplication:

$13 \cdot 1 = 13$

$c \cdot 1 = c$

Examples of Inverse Operations and Reciprocals:

$a + (-a) = 0$

$a \cdot \dfrac{1}{a} = 1$

Name: _____ Date: _____

Chapter 4: Properties (cont.)

Practice: Identity and Inverse Properties of Addition and Multiplication

Directions: Use the identity or inverse properties of addition or multiplication to solve the following.

1. $432 \cdot$ _____ $= 1$

2. $0.23 \cdot$ _____ $= 1$

3. _____ $\cdot 10{,}000 = 1$

4. $-2{,}342 +$ _____ $= 0$

5. $392 + (-566) + 182 + (-392) + (-182) + 566 =$ _____

6. $392 + (-566) +$ _____ $= -182 + 392 + 182 + (-566)$

7. $\frac{147}{213} \cdot$ _____ $= 1$

8. _____ $\cdot 3.5 = 1$

9. $0 = x + (x + y) + (y + z) +$ _____

10. $\frac{0.15}{4} \cdot$ _____ $= 1$

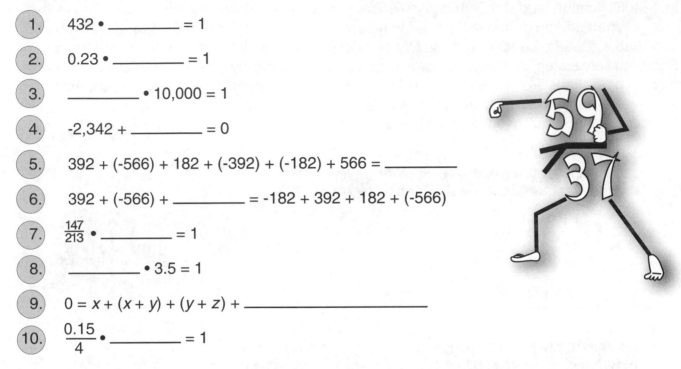

Challenge Problems: Identity and Inverse Properties of Addition and Multiplication

1. $(438 + 951 - 17) \cdot$ _____ $= 1$

2. Yasmine thought that the multiplicative inverse of 0.33 would be 0.67. Why do you think she said that, and do you agree with her? _____

_____

3. $\frac{117}{23} \cdot \frac{}{117} \cdot \frac{59}{37} \cdot \frac{23}{59} = 1$

4. $3.5 \cdot \dfrac{1}{\text{_____}} = 1$

5. $\frac{0}{13} \cdot$ _____ $= 1$

Name: _____ Date: _____

Chapter 4: Properties (cont.)

Basic Overview: Commutative Properties of Addition and Multiplication

The Commutative Property of Addition states that no matter the order in which you add two numbers, the sum is always the same. The Commutative Property of Multiplication states that no matter the order in which you multiply two numbers, the answer is always the same.

Examples of the Commutative Property of Addition:

$5 + 6 = 6 + 5$

$b + c = c + b$

Examples of the Commutative Property of Multiplication:

$3 \cdot 8 = 8 \cdot 3$

$b \cdot a = a \cdot b$

$20 \cdot \frac{1}{2} = \frac{1}{2} \cdot 20$

$c \cdot \frac{1}{d} = \frac{1}{d} \cdot c$

Practice: Commutative Properties of Addition and Multiplication

Directions: Fill in each blank and, if possible, tell whether the example is showing the Commutative Property of Addition or the Commutative Property of Multiplication.

1. $456 \cdot (123 + 223) =$ ____346____ $\cdot 456$ M

2. $(897 + 909) + (233 + 478) = (233 + 478) +$ __897+909__   A

3. ____22____ $+ 99 \cdot 86 = 99 \cdot 86 + 22$ A

4. $s \cdot [(a + b) + (c + 9)] = s \cdot [(c + 9) + ($ __a+b__ $)]$ A

5. $(\frac{1}{5} \cdot 7) + \frac{1}{5} \cdot 9 = \frac{1}{5} \cdot 9 +$ __$\frac{1}{5} \times 7$__   M

6. $319 \cdot ($ __98+83__ $) = (98 + 83) \cdot 319$ M

Name: _____ Date: _____

Chapter 4: Properties (cont.)

7. $33a + 19b \cdot 41z =$ _____ *19b* $\cdot 41z + 33a$ _____

8. $(37a + 49b) \cdot (9z + 2c) = (9z + 2c) \cdot$ _____ *49b + 37a* _____

9. (_____) $\cdot 0.62a + 56b = 56b + (3.2m + 53) \cdot 0.62a$ _____

10. $((98 + 17b + 54 + 31 + 9) + 81)a = (81 + ($_____$))a$ _____

Challenge Problems: Commutative Properties of Addition and Multiplication

1. $912 +$ _____ $=$ _____ $+ 912$

2. Using only mental arithmetic, determine which of the following values is the largest.
    $\frac{1}{5} \cdot 87{,}263$ or $87{,}263 \cdot \frac{2}{7}$ How do you know? _____

    _____

3. Using only the numbers 1, 2, 3, 4, and 5, place numbers in the appropriate places to demonstrate the Commutative Property of Addition.

    (_____ + _____) $\cdot$ _____ $=$ (_____ + _____) $\cdot$ _____

4. Using only the numbers 1, 2, 3, 4, and 5, place numbers in the appropriate places to demonstrate the Commutative Property of Multiplication.

    (_____ + _____) $\cdot$ _____ $=$ _____ $\cdot$ (_____ + _____)

5. Rewrite the following expression using the Commutative Property of Multiplication.

    $3 \cdot ((4s + 3n) \cdot (9a + 2)) =$ _____

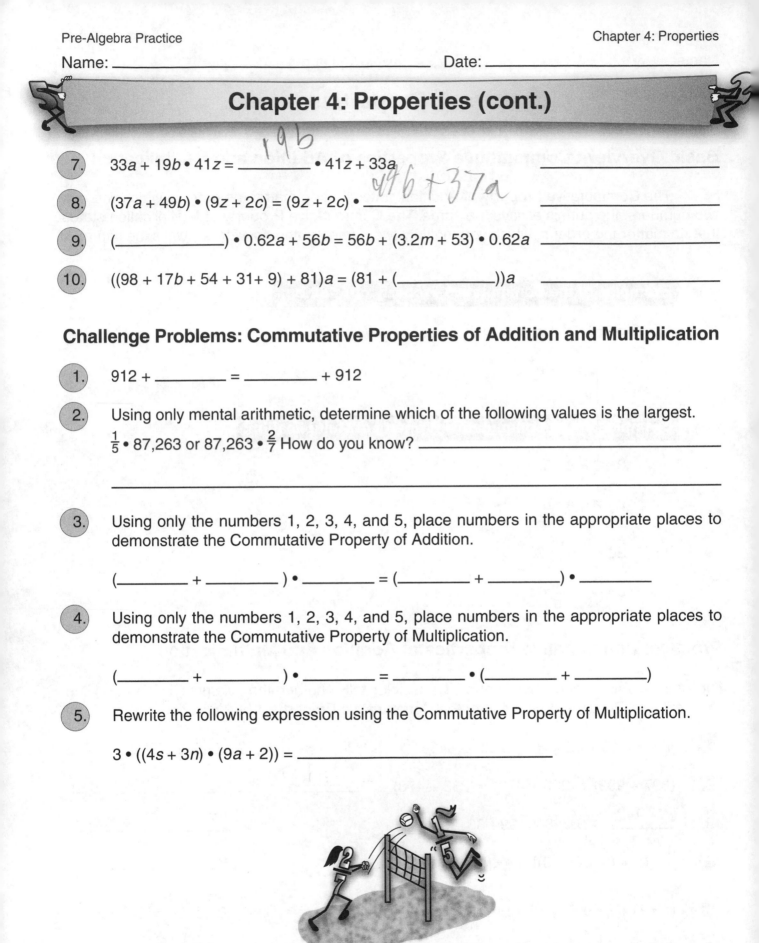

Name: _____ Date: _____

Chapter 4: Properties (cont.)

Basic Overview: Associative Properties of Addition and Multiplication

The Associative Property of Addition states that no matter the order in which you group three numbers, the sum will always be the same. The Associative Property of Multiplication states that no matter the order in which you group three numbers, the answer will always be the same.

Examples of the Associative Property of Addition:

$(5 + 6) + 7 = 5 + (6 + 7)$

$(a + b) + c = a + (b + c)$

Examples of the Associative Property of Multiplication:

$(5 \cdot 4) \cdot 8 = 5 \cdot (4 \cdot 8)$

$(x \cdot y) \cdot z = x \cdot (y \cdot z)$

Practice: Associative Properties of Addition and Multiplication

Directions: Fill in each blank and, if possible, tell whether the example is showing the Associative Property of Addition or the Associative Property of Multiplication.

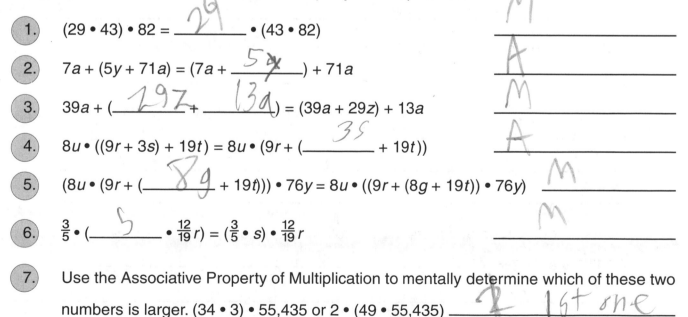

1. $(29 \cdot 43) \cdot 82 = \underline{\quad 29 \quad} \cdot (43 \cdot 82)$ M

2. $7a + (5y + 71a) = (7a + \underline{\quad 5y \quad}) + 71a$ A

3. $39a + (\underline{\quad 29z \quad} + \underline{\quad 13a \quad}) = (39a + 29z) + 13a$ M

4. $8u \cdot ((9r + 3s) + 19t) = 8u \cdot (9r + (\underline{\quad 3s \quad} + 19t))$ A

5. $(8u \cdot (9r + (\underline{\quad 8g \quad} + 19t))) \cdot 76y = 8u \cdot ((9r + (8g + 19t)) \cdot 76y)$ M

6. $\frac{3}{5} \cdot (\underline{\quad s \quad} \cdot \frac{12}{19}r) = (\frac{3}{5} \cdot s) \cdot \frac{12}{19}r$ M

7. Use the Associative Property of Multiplication to mentally determine which of these two numbers is larger. $(34 \cdot 3) \cdot 55{,}435$ or $2 \cdot (49 \cdot 55{,}435)$ _____ 1st one

Name: _____ Date: _____

Chapter 4: Properties (cont.)

8. Use the Associative Property of Multiplication to mentally determine the following.

$(\frac{37}{59} \cdot \frac{2}{7}) \cdot 3.5 =$ _____

9. Ohara claimed he did the following computation using the Associative Property of Addition. Do you agree? Why? $(27 + 63) + 3 = (27 + 3) + 63 = 30 + 63 = 93$.

yes _____

10. Use the Associative Property of Addition to mentally compute the following.

$(87 + 981) + 19 =$ *1000 + 87* _____

Challenge Problems: Associative Properties of Addition and Multiplication

1. Using only the numbers 1, 2, 3, 4, and 5, place numbers in the appropriate places to demonstrate the Associative Property of Multiplication.

(_____ + _____) • _____ • _____ = ((_____ + _____) • _____)

• _____

2. Ariel thought that the following was an example of the Associative Property of Addition. Do you agree? Explain your answer. $53 + (19 + (24 + 16)) = 53 + (19 + (16 + 24))$

yes because its Assosiative _____

_____

3. Complete the sentence using an appropriate Associative Property.

$(5 \cdot ((3 + 4) + 7)) \cdot 9 =$ *14 X 45* _____

4. Explain how to mentally compute the following by using the Associative Property of Multiplication. $(78{,}923{,}234 \cdot 2) \cdot 5$

189233320 = 78923234 × 10 _____

5. Explain how to mentally compute the following by using the Associative Property of Addition. $\frac{3}{5} + (-\frac{3}{5} + \frac{12}{19})$ *3/5 + 3/5 + 12/19 = 0 + 12/19*

_____

Chapter 4: Properties (cont.)

Basic Overview: Distributive Properties

The Distributive Property states that when you have both the operation of addition and the operation of multiplication to perform, you can decide which to do first.

Examples of the Distributive Properties:

$$12(6 + 5) = 12(6) + 12(5)$$

$$a(b + c) = a(b) + a(c)$$

Practice: Distributive Properties

1. $48 \cdot (18 + \underline{45 \times 93}) = 48 \cdot 18 + 48 \cdot 93$

2. $(40 + 8) \cdot 18 = (40 \cdot 18) + (\underline{8} \cdot 18)$

3. Is the following a true statement? $52 \cdot (25 - 8) = (52 \cdot 25) - (52 \cdot 8)$

   yes

4. Use the Distributive Property to mentally simplify. $(3 \cdot 15) + (3 \cdot 5)$

   _60_

5. Use the Distributive Property to change this addition situation into a multiplication situation. $32a + 18a$

   _A 50_

6. Is the following a true statement? $(36 + 18) \div 6 = (36 \div 6) + (18 \div 6)$

   yes

7. $(72 \cdot 13) + (72 \cdot \text{-}13) = \underline{72 \times 13} \cdot (13 + \text{-}13)$

8. Show how to use the Distributive Property of Multiplication Over Addition to easily compute the following. $(981 \cdot 53) + (19 \cdot 53)$

   _____

Name: _____ Date: _____

Chapter 4: Properties (cont.)

9. Show how to use the Distributive Property of Multiplication Over Subtraction to easily compute the following. $(819 \cdot 50) - (19 \cdot 50)$

   _____

10. $(3a \cdot 3b) + (3a \cdot 4c) = 3a \cdot ($ _____ + _____ $)$

11. Simplify $30 \cdot (20 + 4)$ using the Distributive Property of Multiplication Over Addition.

    _____

12. Simplify $(\frac{1}{5} \cdot 31) + (\frac{1}{5} \cdot 14)$ using the Distributive Property of Multiplication Over Addition.

    _____

13. Rewrite $9a + 12b$ using the Distributive Property. _____

14. Rewrite $43a^5 + 9a^2$ using the Distributive Property. _____

15. Rewrite $-8z^2 + 4z$ using the Distributive Property. _____

Challenge Problems: Distributive Properties

1. Use the Distributive Property to mentally compute the following. $42 \cdot (\frac{3}{7} + \frac{5}{21})$.

   _____

2. Does multiplication also distribute over subtraction? That is, is $a \cdot (b - c) = a \cdot b - a \cdot c$ always true? _____

3. Use the Distributive Property to mentally compute $48 \cdot 12$. _____

4. Use the Distributive Property to mentally compute $\frac{5}{17} \cdot (34 + 85)$.

   _____

5. Using only the numbers 1, 3, 4, 6 or 7, complete the following to show the Distributive Property of Multiplication Over Addition.

   (_____ + _____) • _____ = (_____ • _____) + (_____ • _____)

6. Use the Distributive Property of Multiplication Over Addition to compute. $\frac{3}{7} \cdot (\frac{14}{3} + \frac{28}{9})$

   _____

Name: _____ Date: _____

Chapter 4: Properties (cont.)

Checking Progress: All Properties

Directions: Which property is it? Write the name of the property that is being shown by the following examples.

1. $8 + 0 = 8$

    1. _____

2. $34 \cdot (28 \cdot 99) = 34 \cdot (99 \cdot 28)$

    2. _____

3. $1 = \frac{3}{5} \cdot \frac{5}{3}$

    3. _____

4. $19 \cdot 8 + 19 \cdot 2 = 19 \cdot (8 + 2)$

    4. _____

5. $19 \cdot 28 - 19 \cdot 8 = 19 \cdot (28 - 8)$

    5. _____

6. $(12 + 7) + 13 = 12 + (7 + 13)$

    6. _____

7. $(12 + 7) + 13 = (7 + 12) + 13$

    7. _____

8. $28,376 = 28,376 \cdot 1$

    8. _____

9. $28,376 \cdot (\frac{13}{53} \cdot \frac{53}{13}) = 28,376$

    9. _____

10. $42 \cdot (\frac{3}{7} + \frac{5}{21}) = 42 \cdot \frac{3}{7} + 42 \cdot \frac{5}{21}$

    10. _____

11. $98 + [13 + (-13)] = 98$

    11. _____

12. $98 = 98 + 0$

    12. _____

Name: _____ Date: _____

Chapter 4: Properties (cont.)

13. $\frac{5}{17} \cdot (34 + 95) = \frac{5}{17} \cdot (95 + 34)$ ¹²⁹

13. _____

14. $(52 - 23) \cdot 10 = (52 \cdot 10) - (23 \cdot 10)$

14. _____

15. $(-986{,}553 + 986{,}553) \cdot 45{,}334 = 0 \cdot 45{,}334$

15. _____

16. $(47 + 19) + 21 = 47 + (19 + 21)$

16. _____

17. $(54 \cdot 19) \cdot 987 = (19 \cdot 54) \cdot 987$

17. _____

18. $(3 \cdot \frac{1}{3}) + 63 = 1 + 63$

18. _____

19. $3a(19 + 2a) = (3a \cdot 19) + (3a \cdot 2a)$

19. =dis _____

20. $(48 - 26) \cdot 5 = (48 \cdot 5) - (26 \cdot 5)$

20. #Dis _____

Chapter 5: Exponents and Exponential Expressions

Basic Overview: Exponents and Exponential Expressions

Rather than having to write out repeated multiplication, symbols called **exponents** can be used as shorthand notation to indicate that action. The exponent indicates how many times the number is used as a factor. The **square of a number** means to use the number as a factor twice. The **cube of a number** means to use the number as a factor three times. In the exponential expression 4^3, the 4 is the base, and the 3 is the exponent. 4^3 is the same as $4 \cdot 4 \cdot 4$. Since there are no parentheses, start at the left and move right: $4 \cdot 4 = 16$, $16 \cdot 4 = 64$, so $4^3 = 64$.

Example of an Exponent:

7^2 (means 7 squared, or 7 raised to the second power)

$7 \cdot 7 = 49$

So $7^2 = 49$

Examples of Algebraic Expressions With Exponents:

$3x^5$

$(5x^3y)^4$

Examples of Rules to Simplify Expressions With Exponents:

Multiplication Rule $a^m \cdot a^n = a^{m+n}$

Division Rule $a^m \div a^n = a^{m-n}$

Power to a Power Rule $(a^m)^n = a^{m \cdot n}$

Name: _____ Date: _____

Chapter 5: Exponents and Exponential Expressions (cont.)

Practice: Exponential Expressions

Directions: Evaluate each exponential expression.

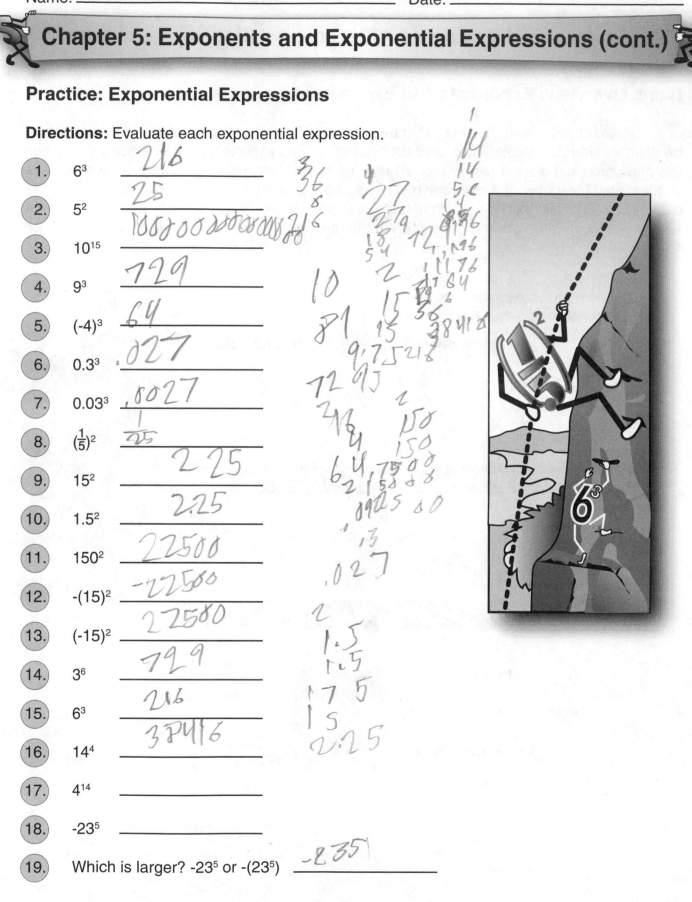

1. 6^3 _____ 216

2. 5^2 _____ 25

3. 10^{15} _____ 1000000000000000

4. 9^3 _____ 729

5. $(-4)^3$ _____ 64

6. 0.3^3 _____ .027

7. 0.03^3 _____ .0027

8. $(\frac{1}{5})^2$ _____ $\frac{1}{25}$

9. 15^2 _____ 225

10. 1.5^2 _____ 2.25

11. 150^2 _____ 22500

12. $-(15)^2$ _____ -22500

13. $(-15)^2$ _____ 22500

14. 3^6 _____ 729

15. 6^3 _____ 216

16. 14^4 _____ 38416

17. 4^{14} _____

18. -23^5 _____

19. Which is larger? -23^5 or $-(23^5)$ _____ -2351

Chapter 5: Exponents and Exponential Expressions (cont.)

20. $(\frac{5}{3})^2$ _____

21. 3.2^5 _____

22. 11^4 _____

23. 111^2 _____

24. $111,111^2$ _____

25. Compute 9^2, 99^2, 999^2, $9,999^2$. From the pattern you see in your solutions, predict the

    solution to $999,999^2$. Was your prediction correct?

    _____

Challenge Problems: Exponential Expressions

1. Barb and Ali had a discussion about the value of the expression

   -5^2. Barb thought this was the same as 25, while Ali said it was

   -25. With whom do you agree?

   barb because a pos times neg equals pos

2. $y^0 =$ ___0___

3. Write the number 64 in exponential form. __8^2__

4. When looking at two exponential expressions, Noah thought that the expression with the

   larger exponent always represented the larger value. Do you agree with Noah? Why or

   why not? _No example $2^5 = 32$ $8^2 = 64$_

   _____

5. Is there an example where $a^b = b^a$? _____

6. What is the largest integer value for b so that $3^b < 4,000$? __1333 3^7__

Name: _____ Date: _____

Chapter 5: Exponents and Exponential Expressions (cont.)

Basic Overview: Multiplying Exponential Expressions With Coefficients

To multiply exponential expressions, first compute the value of the exponential expression, and then multiply by the coefficient.

Examples of Multiplying Exponential Expressions With Coefficients:

$4(5)^2$

$(5)^2 = (5 \cdot 5) = 25$

$4(25)$

$4(5)^2 = 100$

Practice: Multiplying Exponential Expressions With Coefficients

Directions: Evaluate each expression.

1. $3^2 \cdot 5$ _____

2. $5^2(-3)$ _____

3. $10^2(b)$ _____

4. $9^2 \cdot 10$ _____

5. $10^2 \cdot 9$ _____

6. $-5 \cdot 3^5$ _____

7. $3 \cdot -5^5$ _____

8. $10^2(b)^3$ _____

9. $-41^2 \cdot b^{41}$ _____

10. $a^{12} \cdot 4 \cdot 5^2 \cdot 9$ _____

11. $-4 \cdot -3^3$ _____

Chapter 5: Exponents and Exponential Expressions (cont.)

12. $(-4 \cdot -3)^3$ _____

13. $-(4 \cdot -3)^3$ _____

14. $-(4 \cdot 3)^3$ _____

15. $2^2 \cdot 3^2 \cdot 5^2$ _____

16. $(2^2 \cdot 3^2 \cdot 5)^2$ _____

17. $(2^2 \cdot 3)^2 \cdot 5^2$ _____

18. $2^2 \cdot (3^2 \cdot 5)^2$ _____

19. $3 \cdot 10^5 + 4 \cdot 10^5$ _____

20. $8 \cdot 10^5 + 2 \cdot 10^5$ _____

Challenge Problems: Exponential Expressions With Coefficients

1. Jason computed $5 \cdot 3^2$ as follows: $5 \cdot 3 = 15$; $15^2 = 225$. Do you agree with Jason? Why or why not? _No because exponents first_

2. Enrique looked at the expressions, $2^2 \cdot 3^2 \cdot 5^2$ and $(2 \cdot 3 \cdot 5)^2$, and wondered if the two had the same value? What do you think? _Yes_

3. Maria looked at the following expression, $8 \cdot 10^4 + 9 \cdot 10^3 + 4 \cdot 10^2 + 5 \cdot 10^1$, and immediately knew the value. Can you compute this mentally? _____

4. Solve. $0.2 \cdot 0.3^4$ _.00085_

5. Avery looked at the following expression, $2 \cdot 0.1^1 + 3 \cdot 0.1^2 + 1 \cdot 0.1^3 + 5 \cdot 0.1^4 + 2 \cdot 0.1^5$ and immediately knew the value. Can you compute this mentally? _____

Name: _____ Date: _____

Chapter 5: Exponents and Exponential Expressions (cont.)

Basic Overview: Addition and Subtraction of Exponential Expressions With Like Terms

Exponential expressions can be added or subtracted if they have the same base and same exponent by adding or subtracting the coefficient.

Example of Addition and Subtraction of Exponential Expressions With Like Terms:

$4(y^3) + 8(y^3)$

The bases are the same, y, and the exponent ^{3} is the same, so they can be added.

Add the coefficients. $4 + 8 = 12$

$4(y^3) + 8(y^3) = 12y^3$

Practice: Addition and Subtraction of Exponential Expressions With Like Terms

Directions: Evaluate the following expressions.

1. $18(z^3) + 5(z^3)$ _$23z^6$_

2. $9[(4^3) + 4(4^3)]$ _____

3. $15(z^3) - 23(z^3)$ _$-8z^6$_

4. $71(2^3) - 83(2^3)$ _____

5. $1(z^2) - 31(z^2)$ _$-30z^4$_

6. $32a^4 - 19a^4 + 6a^4 - 12a^4$ _____

7. $32a^4 - (19a^4 + 6a^4 - 12a^4)$ _$20a^{16}$_

8. $5^4(9^2) + 5^4(2^3)$ _____

9. $5^4(a^2) + 5^4(a^3)$ _____

10. $42a^2 + 33b^4 - 17a^2 - 34b^4$ _____

11. $42a^2 + 33b^4 - (17a^2 - 34b^4)$ _____

12. $s^5 + s^4 + s^3 - s^5 + s^4 + s^3$ _____

13. $s^5 + s^4 + s^3 - (s^5 + s^4) + s^3$ _____

14. $s^5 + s^4 + s^3 - (s^5 + s^4 + s^3)$ _____

15. $88n^{12} -$ _____ $= 122n^{12}$

16. $a^{15} + b^{15} + c^{15} + 2(a^{15} + b^{15} + c^{15}) + 3(a^{15} + b^{15} + c^{15})$ _____

Name: _____ Date: _____

Chapter 5: Exponents and Exponential Expressions (cont.)

17. $a^{15} + b^{15} + c^{15} + 2a^{15} + 2b^{15} + 2c^{15} + 3a^{15} + 3b^{15} + 3c^{15}$ _____ *15abc^{135} 5a^{45}5b^{45}5c^{45}*

18. $a^{15} + b^{15} + c^{15} + 2(a^{14} + b^{14} + c^{14}) + 3(a^{13} + b^{13} + c^{13})$ _____

19. $2^3a^7 + 3^3a^7 + 4^3a^7 + 5^3a^7$ _____

20. $61 \cdot 7^5 - 58 \cdot 7^5 + 4 \cdot 7^5$ _____

21. $61^2 \cdot 7^5 - 58^2 \cdot 7^5 + 4^2 \cdot 7^5$ _____

22. $(6 \cdot 7)^5 - (8 \cdot 7)^5 + (4 \cdot 7)^5$ _____

23. Is $18^3 - 18^2 = 18$? _____

24. $34^6 \cdot$ _____ $= 34^{13}$

25. For what positive integer values of a is $a^7 \leq 5^7$? _____

Challenge Problems: Addition and Subtraction With Like Terms

1. Evangelina looked at the expression, $3z^2 + 5z$, and rewrote it as $8z^3$. Do you agree with Evangelina? Why or why not? *No she added a power of it*

_____

2. Yuki computed $1^2 + 2^2 + 3^2$ as $(1 + 2 + 3)^2$. Do you agree with Yuki? *No*

3. $54w^8 -$ _____ *38w – 1325* _____ $= 16w^8 + 13z^5$

4. What should be added to $c^{15} + 3a$ to obtain $-3a + c + b^2$?

_____ *-6a + c^5 – b^2* _____

5. For what positive integer values of a will $5a^6 + 3a^4 \leq 2,000$? *6a^6 ≤ 400 – 3a^4*

_____

6. When asked to determine the value of $(6 \cdot 7)^5 - (8 \cdot 7)^5 + (4 \cdot 7)^5$, Macy said she thought you would get the same answer from $[(6 \cdot 7) - (8 \cdot 7) + (4 \cdot 7)]^5$. Do you agree with Macy? Why or why not? *No*

_____

Name: _____ Date: _____

Chapter 5: Exponents and Exponential Expressions (cont.)

Basic Overview: Multiplication and Division of Exponential Expressions

Two exponential expressions can be multiplied if they have the same base. Add the exponents and use this sum with the same base: $(n^2)(n^5) = n^{2+5} = n^7$.

You can divide exponential expressions with the same base. Subtract the denominator exponent from the numerator exponent, and use this difference with the same base $(n^5) \div (n^3) = n^{5-3} = n^2$.

Example of Multiplying Exponential Expressions:

$(5^2)(5^5) =$

Add the exponents. $2 + 5 = 7$

Raise the common base to this exponent. $5^7 = 78,125$

Example of Multiplying Exponential Expressions With Coefficients:

$(3x^2)(5x^5) =$

Multiply the coefficients. $(3)(5) = 15$

Add the exponents. $2 + 5 = 7$

Multiply the factors. $15x^7$

Example of Dividing Exponential Expressions:

$8^5 \div 8^2 =$

Subtract the exponents. $5 - 2 = 3$

Raise the common base to this exponent.

$8^5 \div 8^2 = 8^3$, or 512

Name: _____ Date: _____

Chapter 5: Exponents and Exponential Expressions (cont.)

Practice: Multiplication and Division of Exponential Expressions

Directions: Simplify the expressions using only positive exponents.

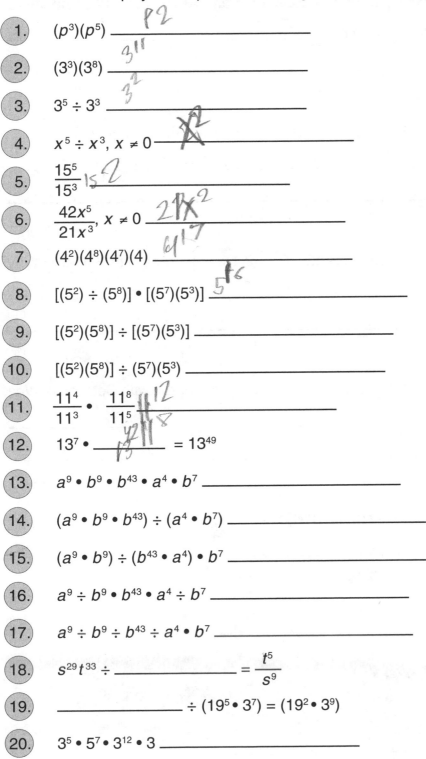

1. $(p^3)(p^5)$ _____ *(handwritten: $P2$)*

2. $(3^3)(3^8)$ _____ *(handwritten: 3^{11})*

3. $3^5 \div 3^3$ _____ *(handwritten: 3^2)*

4. $x^5 \div x^3, \, x \neq 0$ _____ *(handwritten: x^2)*

5. $\dfrac{15^5}{15^3}$ _____ *(handwritten: 15^2)*

6. $\dfrac{42x^5}{21x^3}, \, x \neq 0$ _____ *(handwritten: $21x^2$)*

7. $(4^2)(4^8)(4^7)(4)$ _____ *(handwritten: 4^{17})*

8. $[(5^2) \div (5^8)] \cdot [(5^7)(5^3)]$ _____ *(handwritten: 5^6)*

9. $[(5^2)(5^8)] \div [(5^7)(5^3)]$ _____

10. $[(5^2)(5^8)] \div (5^7)(5^3)$ _____

11. $\dfrac{11^4}{11^3} \cdot \dfrac{11^8}{11^5}$ _____ *(handwritten: 11^{12})*

12. $13^7 \cdot$ _____ $= 13^{49}$

13. $a^9 \cdot b^9 \cdot b^{43} \cdot a^4 \cdot b^7$ _____

14. $(a^9 \cdot b^9 \cdot b^{43}) \div (a^4 \cdot b^7)$ _____

15. $(a^9 \cdot b^9) \div (b^{43} \cdot a^4) \cdot b^7$ _____

16. $a^9 \div b^9 \cdot b^{43} \cdot a^4 \div b^7$ _____

17. $a^9 \div b^9 \div b^{43} \div a^4 \cdot b^7$ _____

18. $s^{29} t^{33} \div$ _____ $= \dfrac{t^5}{s^9}$

19. _____ $\div (19^5 \cdot 3^7) = (19^2 \cdot 3^9)$

20. $3^5 \cdot 5^7 \cdot 3^{12} \cdot 3$ _____

Name: _____ Date: _____

Chapter 5: Exponents and Exponential Expressions (cont.)

Challenge Problems: Multiplying and Dividing Exponential Expressions

1. Anna thought that the following two expressions, $(3^2)^4$ and $(3^4)^2$, gave the same value. Do you agree with Anna? Why or why not? _____

   _____

2. Reed thought that $13^5 \cdot 13^7 = 13^{35}$. Do you agree with Reed? Why or why not? *No because he's multiplying 2 exponents* *not numbers*

3. Richard thought that $\dfrac{11^{42}}{11^{21}} = 11^2$ because $42 \div 21 = 2$. Do you agree with Richard? Why or why not? *No*

   _____

4. Courtney thought that $\dfrac{11^{42}}{11^{-42}} = 0$ because $42 - 42 = 0$. Do you agree with Courtney? Why or why not? _____

   _____

5. Find all positive integer values of s so that $3^5 \cdot 3^s \geq 20,000$.

   _____

$3^5 \cdot 3^s \geq 20,000$

Soapbox Special $13^5 \cdot 13^7 = 13^{12}$

Chapter 5: Exponents and Exponential Expressions (cont.)

Basic Overview: Raising to a Power, Including Negative Exponents

To change an exponential expression to a higher power, multiply the exponents. To solve problems with negative exponents, find the reciprocal of a number. When you find the reciprocal of a number, you make the numerator the denominator and the denominator the numerator. Change the negative exponents to reciprocals by taking the reciprocal of the number that is raised to a power and change the exponent to a positive number.

Example of Raising the Exponential Power:

$(2^2)^5$

Multiply the exponents. $2 \cdot 5 = 10$

$(2^2)^5 = 2^{10} = 1{,}024$

Example of Reciprocals:

The reciprocal of $\frac{1}{2}$ is $\frac{2}{1}$.

Example of Solving Problems With Negative Exponents:

5^{-2}

Find the reciprocal of the number that is raised to a power.

$5 = \frac{5}{1}$ so the reciprocal is $\frac{1}{5}$.

Change the exponent in the reciprocal to a positive number.

$5^{-2} = \left(\frac{1}{5}\right)^2 = \frac{1^2}{5^2} = \frac{1}{5^2}$

Name: _____ Date: _____

Chapter 5: Exponents and Exponential Expressions (cont.)

Practice: Raising to a Power, Including Negative Exponents

Directions: Simplify each expression using only positive exponents unless otherwise stated.

1. $(3^2)^6$ _____ 3^{12}

2. $(7^{29})^0$ _____ 0

3. $(2^3)^3$ _____ 2^4

4. $(x^5)^2$ _____ x^{10}

5. Rewrite 5^{-4} using only positive exponents. The value is _____.

6. Rewrite 2^{-5} using only positive exponents. The value is _____.

7. $(((7)^2)^5)^3$ _____

8. Which is greater? $\left(\frac{1}{3}\right)^2$ or 3^{-2} _____ $\frac{1}{3} \, 2$ _____

9. Rewrite $(5^2)^{-1}$ using only positive exponents. The value is $\frac{1}{5^2}$ _____.

10. $(61^{-2})^{-3}$ _____

11. Alicia wonders if $(-13)^2$ and 13^{-2} are the same. What do you think? _____

_____

12. $\left(\frac{13^{-3}}{43^{-2}}\right)$ _____

13. $(((1)^2)^3)^4$ _____ 1^{24}

14. $(((1)^{-2})^3)^4$ _____

15. $(((-1)^2)^3)^4$ _____

16. Rewrite -2^{-5} using only positive exponents. The value is _____.

17. Rewrite $-(2)^{-8}$ using only positive exponents. The value is _____.

18. Rewrite $\left(\frac{1}{-2}\right)^{-7}$ using only positive exponents. The value is _____.

19. $((y^2)^3)^{25}$ _____

20. $((2^2)^3)^{25}$ _____

Name: _____   Date: _____

Chapter 5: Exponents and Exponential Expressions (cont.)

Challenge Problems: Raising to a Power, Including Negative Exponents

1. Which is larger? $\left(\frac{1}{5}\right)^{-3}$ or 5^2 _____

2. Makenzie thought the value of $\left(\frac{1}{-4}\right)^3$ was $\left(\frac{1}{-64}\right)$, and Jensen thought the value was -12. With whom do you agree, if either? Why? _____

_____

3. Eric thought the value of $\left(\frac{1}{-4}\right)^{-3}$ was 64, while Emil thought the value was -64. With whom do you agree, if either? Why? _____

_____

4. Olga thought that $(7^3)^{-3} = 7^0 = 1$. Do you agree with Olga? Why or why not?

_____

_____

5. Find the value of x if $(((3^2)^3)^x) = 3^{42}$. _____

Name: _____ Date: _____

Chapter 5: Exponents and Exponential Expressions (cont.)

Basic Overview: Scientific Notation

Scientists use both very large and very small numbers. To make numbers easier to work with, they use scientific notation. Scientific notation uses powers of ten. For example, $10^2 = 100$ or $10^{-3} = 0.001$. They would write the number 1,000,000 like this: $1 \cdot 10^6$ or 1 times $10 \cdot 10 \cdot 10 \cdot 10 \cdot 10 \cdot 10$. Each number written in scientific notation is written as a number, called a coefficient, which is greater than or equal to 1 and less than 10 ($1 \le a < 10$), multiplied by some power of ten.

Examples of Scientific Notation:

10^8 is 10 raised to the 8th power

10 times itself 8 times or
$10 \cdot 10 \cdot 10 \cdot 10 \cdot 10 \cdot 10 \cdot 10 \cdot 10 = $
100,000,000

$10^8 = 100,000,000$

$64 \cdot 10^{-4} = $

64 divided by 10 four times
$64 \div 10 \div 10 \div 10 \div 10 = $
0.0064

or $64 \cdot 0.0001 = 0.0064$

When changing a number to scientific notation, just remember to count the number of decimal places the decimal is moved. That number becomes the exponent.

If you move the decimal to the left, it is a positive exponent. $37,809 = 3.7809 \cdot 10^4$

If you move the decimal to the right, it is a negative exponent. $0.0009516 = 9.516 \cdot 10^{-4}$

Practice: Scientific Notation

1.) What number is represented by $4.324 \cdot 10^9$? _____

2.) What number is represented by $123.12324 \cdot 10^5$? Write this number in scientific notation.

_____   _____

3.) Write 0.003404 in scientific notation. _____

4.) Which of these numbers is the larger? $34.561 \cdot 10^{-3}$ or $0.0034561 \cdot 10^2$ _____

5.) Write 4,399.23 in scientific notation. _____

6.) Write $5,784 \cdot 2,200$ in scientific notation. _____

Name: _____ Date: _____

Chapter 5: Exponents and Exponential Expressions (cont.)

7. Write $5.784 \cdot 2.2$ in scientific notation. _____

8. Write $(5.784 \cdot 10^5) \cdot (2.2 \cdot 10^{-8})$ in scientific notation. _____

9. Find the value of t if $9.999999 \cdot 10^t = 99999.99$. _____

10. Find the value of t if $88.888 \cdot 10^t = 0.00088888$. _____

11. What number is represented by $123.12324 \cdot 10^{-5}$? Write this number in scientific notation.

    _____

12. What number is represented by $48.2992 \cdot 10^4$? Write this number in scientific notation.

    _____

13. Write $2 \cdot 3 \cdot 4 \cdot 5 \cdot 6 \cdot 7 \cdot 8$ in scientific notation. _____

14. Find z if $6 \cdot 8 \cdot 90 \cdot 12 = z \cdot 10^2$ _____

15. Find z if $4 \cdot 9 \cdot 12 \cdot z = 6.048 \cdot 10^3$ _____

Challenge Problems: Scientific Notation

1. Write $\frac{1}{256}$ in scientific notation. _____

2. Write $\frac{5}{16}$ in scientific notation. _____

3. Write $\frac{0.09}{200}$ in scientific notation. _____

4. Write $\frac{(222.5)(10^5)}{(4)(10^2)}$ in scientific notation. _____

5. Write $\frac{(222.5)(10^2)}{(0.04)(10^5)}$ in scientific notation. _____

Chapter 5: Exponents and Exponential Expressions (cont.)

Checking Progress: Exponents and Exponential Expressions

1. Evaluate. 0.02^5 _____

2. Evaluate. -4^3 _____

3. What is the largest integer value for b so that $b^3 < 4{,}000$? _____

4. Evaluate. $8^2 \cdot 10$ _____

5. Evaluate. $(-2 \cdot -3)^3$ _____

6. Combine terms. $42a^2 - 33b^4 - 17a^2 - 34b^4$ _____

7. Combine terms. $42a^2 - (33b^4 - (17a^2 - 34b^4))$ _____

8. Combine terms. $a^{14} \cdot b^{91} \cdot b^7 \cdot a^{41} \cdot b^2$ _____

9. Rewrite 2^{-4} using only positive exponents. The value is _____.

10. Combine terms. $((y^2)^2)^{25}$ _____

11. Write the following in scientific notation. $57.84 \cdot 2.21$ _____

12. Find the value of t if $8.8888 \cdot 10^t = 0.00088888.$ _____

Name: _____ Date: _____

Chapter 6: Square Roots

Basic Overview: Square Numbers and Roots

Four is a square number because two multiplied by two equals four. A **square root** of a number is found by finding out what number, used as a factor twice, equals that given number. Perfect squares are numbers that have a square root that is an integer. The square root of an imperfect square is not an integer. The symbol ≈ means "is approximately" and is used because the number has been rounded off to provide an estimate of the exact root value. Every number has two square roots—a positive square root and a negative square root.

Example of a Square Number:

$25 = 5 \cdot 5$ 25 is a square number.

Example of Square Numbers and Roots:

What number multiplied by itself equals 25?

5 because $5 \cdot 5 = 25$. Also -5, because $(-5) \cdot (-5) = 25$.

Example of a Perfect Square:

100

$\sqrt{100} = 10$

Example of an Imperfect Square:

$\sqrt{3} \approx 1.732$

Name: _____ Date: _____

Chapter 6: Square Roots (cont.)

Rules for Simplifying Radical Expressions

- In simplifying radical expressions: if two numbers are multiplied under the radical sign, you may separate the two expressions. Find the square roots of each and multiply the solutions.

- If two radical expressions are multiplied together, they can be written as products under the same radical sign.

- You may also find factors for the number under the radical and take the square root of the factors.

- If two numbers are divided under a radical sign, they can be separated into two radicals.

- Multiplying the numerator and denominator of a radical expression by the same non-zero number does not change the value.

- Radical expressions can be added and subtracted if each index is the same and each number under the radical sign is the same. The index is the small number in the crook of the radical sign. It tells what root you are looking for ($\sqrt[2]{4}$ means "the square root of 4," $\sqrt[3]{9}$ means "the cube root of 9").

- Radical expressions can be written as fractional exponents. The numerator is the power of the number under the radical sign, and the denominator is the number that is the index.

- Fractional exponents can be changed into radical expressions. The numerator is the exponent of the number under the radical sign, and the denominator is the index.

- Radical expressions are not simplified if there is a radical in the denominator.

Examples of Simplifying Radical Expressions:

If two numbers are multiplied under the radical sign, you may separate the two expressions.

$$\sqrt{(4)(9)}$$

$$(\sqrt{4})(\sqrt{9})$$

$$\sqrt{4} = 2 \quad \sqrt{9} = 3$$

$$(2)(3) = 6$$

$$\sqrt{(4)(9)} = 6$$

Name: _____ Date: _____

Chapter 6: Square Roots (cont.)

Examples of Simplifying Radical Expressions:

If two radical expressions are multiplied together, they can be written as products under the same radical sign.

$$(\sqrt{3})(\sqrt{27}) =$$

$$\sqrt{(3)(27)} =$$

$$\sqrt{81} =$$

$$9$$

Find factors for the number under the radical and take the square root of the factors.

$$\sqrt{18}$$

$$\sqrt{(2)(9)}$$

$$\sqrt{(2)(9)} = (\sqrt{2})(\sqrt{9})$$

$$\sqrt{(2)(9)} = (3\sqrt{2})$$

$$\sqrt{(2)(9)} \approx 3 \cdot 1.414$$

Note that this is $\approx$ and not $=$, because the number has been rounded.

$$\sqrt{(2)(9)} \approx 4.2426$$

If two numbers are divided under a radical sign, they can be separated into two radicals.

$$\sqrt{\frac{9}{4}}$$

$$\frac{\sqrt{9}}{\sqrt{4}}$$

$$\sqrt{9} = 3 \quad \sqrt{4} = 2$$

$$\sqrt{\frac{9}{4}} = \frac{3}{2}$$

Name: _____ Date: _____

Chapter 6: Square Roots (cont.)

Examples of Simplifying Radical Expressions:

Multiplying the numerator and denominator of a radical expression by the same number does not change the value.

$$\frac{5}{\sqrt{3}} =$$

$$\left(\frac{5}{\sqrt{3}}\right)\left(\frac{\sqrt{3}}{\sqrt{3}}\right) =$$

$$\left(\frac{5}{\sqrt{3}}\right)\left(\frac{\sqrt{3}}{\sqrt{3}}\right) = \frac{5\sqrt{3}}{\sqrt{3(3)}} = \frac{5\sqrt{3}}{\sqrt{9}}$$

$$\frac{5}{\sqrt{3}} = \frac{5\sqrt{3}}{\sqrt{9}} = \frac{5\sqrt{3}}{3}$$

Practice: Square Roots

Directions: Simplify each expression. Remember, a radical is not simplified if it has a radical in the denominator.

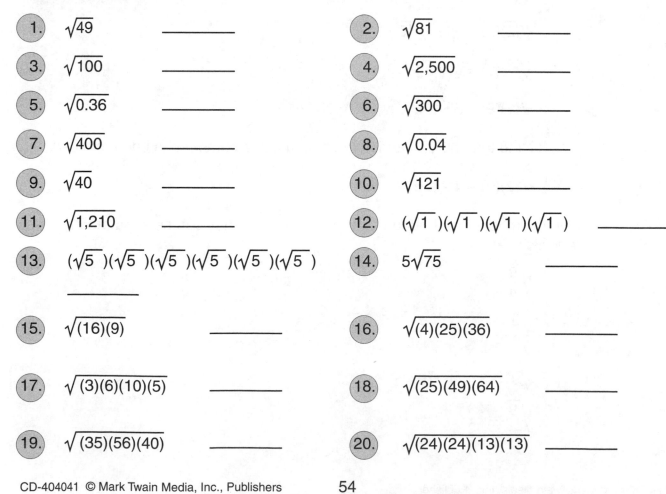

1. $\sqrt{49}$ _____

2. $\sqrt{81}$ _____

3. $\sqrt{100}$ _____

4. $\sqrt{2,500}$ _____

5. $\sqrt{0.36}$ _____

6. $\sqrt{300}$ _____

7. $\sqrt{400}$ _____

8. $\sqrt{0.04}$ _____

9. $\sqrt{40}$ _____

10. $\sqrt{121}$ _____

11. $\sqrt{1,210}$ _____

12. $(\sqrt{1})(\sqrt{1})(\sqrt{1})(\sqrt{1})$ _____

13. $(\sqrt{5})(\sqrt{5})(\sqrt{5})(\sqrt{5})(\sqrt{5})(\sqrt{5})$ _____

14. $5\sqrt{75}$ _____

15. $\sqrt{(16)(9)}$ _____

16. $\sqrt{(4)(25)(36)}$ _____

17. $\sqrt{(3)(6)(10)(5)}$ _____

18. $\sqrt{(25)(49)(64)}$ _____

19. $\sqrt{(35)(56)(40)}$ _____

20. $\sqrt{(24)(24)(13)(13)}$ _____

Name: _____ Date: _____

Chapter 6: Square Roots (cont.)

21. $\sqrt{16z^2}$, $z > 0$ _____

22. $\sqrt{16z^4}$, $z > 0$ _____

23. $\sqrt{16z^6}$, $z > 0$ _____

24. $\sqrt{16z^{13}}$, $z > 0$ _____

25. $\sqrt{81y^{22}}$, $y > 0$ _____

26. $\sqrt{x^4y^2}$, $x > 0, y > 0$ _____

27. $\sqrt{64x^6y^4z^8}$, $x > 0, y > 0, z > 0$ _____

28. $\sqrt{(64)(42)(21)(8)x^6y^4z^8}$, $x > 0, y > 0, z > 0$ _____

29. $(\sqrt{z})(\sqrt{z})$, $z > 0$ _____

30. $(\sqrt{z^3})(\sqrt{z})(\sqrt{z^3})(\sqrt{z^3})$, $z > 0$ _____

31. $(\sqrt{xz^3})(\sqrt{x^3z^5})$, $x > 0, z > 0$ _____

32. $(x\sqrt{z^3})(z\sqrt{x^3z^2})$, $x > 0, z > 0$ _____

33. $(\sqrt{xy})(\sqrt{yz})(\sqrt{xz})$, $x > 0, y > 0, z > 0$ _____

34. $\sqrt{x^2y^2z^2}$, $x > 0, y > 0, z > 0$ _____

35. $(\sqrt{xy})^2$, $x > 0, y > 0$ _____

36. $\sqrt{(2^3)(3^5)(7^2)}$ _____

37. $(\sqrt{3})(\sqrt{6})$ _____

38. $(\sqrt{10})(\sqrt{6})$ _____

39. $(\sqrt{6})(\sqrt{15})(\sqrt{10})$ _____

40. $(\sqrt{6})(\sqrt{15})(\sqrt{10})(\sqrt{6})$ _____

41. $(\sqrt{42})(\sqrt{7})$ _____

42. $(\sqrt{3})(\sqrt{6})$ _____

43. $(5\sqrt{2})(7\sqrt{2})$ _____

44. $(5\sqrt{2})(\sqrt{7})$ _____

45. $(2\sqrt{5})(14\sqrt{15})$ _____

46. $(2\sqrt{2}) \cdot$ _____ $= 6\sqrt{10}$

47. $\sqrt{27}$ _____

48. $\sqrt{8}$ _____

Name: _____ Date: _____

Chapter 6: Square Roots (cont.)

49. $\sqrt{125}$ _____   **50.** $\sqrt{28}$ _____

51. $\sqrt{7^5}$ _____   **52.** $\sqrt{98}$ _____

53. $\sqrt{48}$ _____   **54.** $\sqrt{45}$ _____

55. $\sqrt{5^9}$ _____   **56.** $\sqrt{\frac{36}{25}}$ _____

57. $\sqrt{\frac{81}{16}}$ _____   **58.** $\sqrt{\frac{16}{3}}$ _____

59. $(\sqrt{\frac{49}{16}})(\sqrt{\frac{25}{64}})$ _____   **60.** $\sqrt{\frac{98}{16}}$ _____

61. $\sqrt{\frac{35}{14}}$ _____   **62.** $\sqrt{\frac{3}{25}}$ _____

63. $\sqrt{\frac{25}{3}}$ _____   **64.** $\sqrt{\frac{36}{7}}$ _____

65. $(\sqrt{\frac{5}{7}})(\sqrt{\frac{5}{7}})$ _____   **66.** $(\sqrt{\frac{5}{7}})(\sqrt{\frac{14}{15}})(\sqrt{\frac{5}{6}})$ _____

67. $\dfrac{\sqrt{48}}{\sqrt{5}}$ _____   **68.** $\dfrac{\sqrt{35}}{\sqrt{42}}$ _____

69. $\dfrac{\sqrt{44}}{\sqrt{45}}$ _____   **70.** $(\dfrac{\sqrt{4}}{\sqrt{5}})(\dfrac{\sqrt{24}}{\sqrt{10}})(\dfrac{\sqrt{66}}{\sqrt{15}})$ _____

Challenge Problems: Simplifying Each Expression

1. $(\sqrt{3})(\sqrt{2})(\sqrt{3})$ _____

2. Mary thought the value of the expressions $\sqrt{\frac{49}{100}}$ and $\sqrt{0.49}$ were the same. Duj said she thought they were not the same. With whom do you agree? Why? _____

_____

Name: _____ Date: _____

Chapter 6: Square Roots (cont.)

3. $\sqrt{0.01}$ _____

4. $\sqrt{(0.1)(0.3)(0.3)(0.1)}$ _____

5. $\sqrt{(0.7)^5}$ _____

Basic Overview: Adding and Subtracting Radicals

Radical expressions can be added and subtracted if each index is the same and each number under the radical sign is the same.

Example:

$$3\sqrt{4} + 4\sqrt{4} =$$

$$3 + 4 = 7$$

$$3\sqrt{4} + 4\sqrt{4} = 7\sqrt{4}$$

Practice: Adding and Subtracting Radicals

1. $3\sqrt{49} + \sqrt{4}$ _____

2. $6\sqrt{x} + 5\sqrt{x}, x > 0$ _____

3. $6\sqrt{x} + 5\sqrt{2x}, x > 0$ _____

4. $18\sqrt{5} - 4\sqrt{5}$ _____

5. $9\sqrt{2y} - 31\sqrt{2y}, y > 0$ _____

6. $\sqrt{8y} + 3\sqrt{2y}, y > 0$ _____

7. $\sqrt{12y^3} + \sqrt{3y}, y > 0$ _____

Name: _____ Date: _____

Chapter 6: Square Roots (cont.)

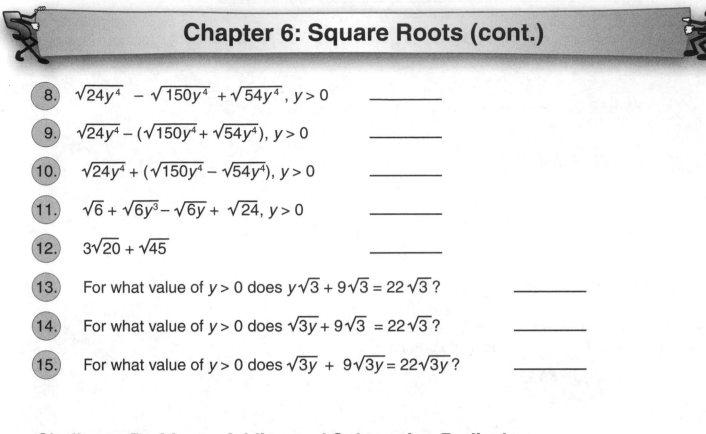

8. $\sqrt{24y^4} - \sqrt{150y^4} + \sqrt{54y^4}$, $y > 0$ _____

9. $\sqrt{24y^4} - (\sqrt{150y^4} + \sqrt{54y^4})$, $y > 0$ _____

10. $\sqrt{24y^4} + (\sqrt{150y^4} - \sqrt{54y^4})$, $y > 0$ _____

11. $\sqrt{6} + \sqrt{6y^3} - \sqrt{6y} + \sqrt{24}$, $y > 0$ _____

12. $3\sqrt{20} + \sqrt{45}$ _____

13. For what value of $y > 0$ does $y\sqrt{3} + 9\sqrt{3} = 22\sqrt{3}$? _____

14. For what value of $y > 0$ does $\sqrt{3y} + 9\sqrt{3} = 22\sqrt{3}$? _____

15. For what value of $y > 0$ does $\sqrt{3y} + 9\sqrt{3y} = 22\sqrt{3y}$? _____

Challenge Problems: Adding and Subtracting Radicals

1. Alena thought the expressions $\sqrt{24y^4} - \sqrt{24y^4} + \sqrt{54y^4}$, $y > 0$, and $\sqrt{24y^4 - 150y^4 + 54y^4}$, $y > 0$ were the same. Do you agree with Alena? Why or why not?

_____

_____

2. $\sqrt{7} + $ _____ $= 3\sqrt{28}$

3. Jill thought the following expressions, $\sqrt{(7)(14)(6)}$ and $14\sqrt{3}$, were equivalent. Do you agree with Jill? Why or why not? _____

_____

4. Len thought that $5\sqrt{3} + 5\sqrt{3} = 10\sqrt{6}$. Do you agree with Len? Why or why not?

_____

_____

5. For what positive values of y will $2\sqrt{22y} > \sqrt{415}$? _____

Name: _____ Date: _____

Chapter 6: Square Roots (cont.)

Checking Progress: Square Roots and Radicals

1. $\sqrt{(25)(49)}$ _____

2. $\sqrt{1,089}$ _____

3. $\sqrt{169z^{14}}$ _____

4. $(a\sqrt{z^9})(z\sqrt{z^4 a^5})$, $a > 0$, $z > 0$ _____

5. $\sqrt{2^5 7^4 23^3}$ _____

6. $(\sqrt{56})(\sqrt{14})$ _____

7. $\dfrac{\sqrt{88}}{\sqrt{143}}$ _____

8. $\left(\dfrac{\sqrt{24}}{\sqrt{15}}\right)\left(\dfrac{\sqrt{50}}{\sqrt{80}}\right)$ _____

9. $13\sqrt{12z} - 2\sqrt{75z}$ _____

10. $5\sqrt{20z} - 4\sqrt{45z}$ _____

Name: _____ Date: _____

Chapter 7: Using Algebra to Generalize Patterns

Basic Overview: Patterns in Number Lists and Tables

Most of mathematics revolves around noticing patterns and using them. For example, all of the properties that were reviewed in earlier sections are the result of patterns. What happens every time you multiply a number by zero? You get zero. That is a pattern that can be observed and generalized into the Zero Multiplication Property. One of the places to look for patterns is in lists of numbers. A table typically shows an input value or number and the related output value or number.

An algebraic expression is a combination of numbers, variables, and operations. Many times, the beginning of work in algebra requires that information (from number lists, tables, or other sources) be put into algebraic form—an expression or equation that describes that situation.

Example of a Pattern in a List:

2, 4, 6, 8, … is the beginning of an infinite list of numbers.

What number would come next in the list? 10

To get the next entry, just add 2 to the previous number in the list.

The nth number in the list will be $n \cdot 2$.

Example of a Pattern in a Table:

Input	Output
3	2
-1	-2
11	10
0	-1

If 7 is the input, what is the output? 6

Take the input number and subtract 1 from it to get the output.

If n is the input number, then $n - 1$ is the output number.

Example of Translating Words Into Symbols:

The number of chairs needed is twice the number of tables.

Let c stand for chairs.

Let t stand for tables.

$c = 2t$

Chapter 7: Using Algebra to Generalize Patterns (cont.)

Practice: Generalizing Patterns in Number Lists and Tables

1. A) Fill in the next numbers in the list. 1, 2, 4, 7, 11, __16__, __22__, __29__, …

   B) Describe, in words, how to find the next numbers in the list. _____
   _____

2. A) Fill in the next numbers in the sequence. 5, 6, 8, 11, 15, __20__, __26__, __~~30~~__, __33__ …

   B) What is the 15th term? _____

3. A) What are the next three terms in the sequence? 1, 2, 1, 2, 1, 2, __1__, __2__, __1__, …

   B) What is the 200th term? _____

   C) What is the 1,000th term? _____

4. What is the 100th term in the sequence? 50, 49, 48, 47, … _____

5. What is the 55th term in the sequence? 3, 6, 9, 12, … _____

6. A) What is the 55th term in the sequence? 1, 55, 3, 110, 5, 165, … _____

   B) What is the 98th term? _____

7. What is the 62nd term in the sequence? 52, 50, 48, 46, … _____

8. The terms in a sequence are given by $3 + 2x$. What are the first 6 terms in the sequence?
   _____

9. The terms in a sequence are given by $(x - 3)^2$. What are the first 10 terms in the sequence?
   _____

10. The terms for one sequence are given by $9 + 7x$, while the terms in another sequence are given by $49 - x$. Will the sequences ever have the same value for a given term number? _____

Name: _____ Date: _____

Chapter 7: Using Algebra to Generalize Patterns (cont.)

Challenge Problems: Patterns in Number Lists

1. A) Fill in the next numbers in the sequence. 1, 4, 9, 16, _____, _____, _____, ...

   B) What is the 30th term? _____

2. A) What are the next three terms in the sequence? 1, 4, 7, 10, 13, _____, _____,

   _____

   B) What is the 200th term? _____

3. A) What are the next three terms in the sequence? 10, 13, 16, 19, _____, _____,

   _____

   B) What is the 200th term? _____

4. What is the 431st term in the sequence? 1, 1, 9, 2, 25, 3, 49, 4, 81, ... _____,

   _____

5. What is the 2,422nd term in the sequence in Challenge Problem 4? _____

Challenge Problems: Generalizing Patterns in Tables

1. For the input/output table:

Input	Output
2	4
0	2
-4	-2
5	7

A) If the input is 21, what is the output? _____

B) If the output is 21, what is the input? _____

C) Describe the rule in words: _____

_____

D) Describe the rule in symbols: if *n* is the input, _____

Chapter 7: Using Algebra to Generalize Patterns (cont.)

2. For the input/output table, find each of the following:

Input	Output
1	3
3	7
-2	-3
-4	-7
0	1

A) If the input is -5, what is the output? _____

B) If 23 is the output, what is the input? _____

C) Describe the rule in words: _____

_____

D) Describe the rule in symbols: if *n* is the input, _____

3. If an input/output table was made with the following rule: 80 minus five times the input gives the output, then ...

A) if the input is 10, what is the output? _____

B) if the output is 0, what is the input? _____

C) describe the rule in symbols: if *n* is the input, _____

4. If an input/output table was made with the following rule, squaring the input and subtracting 3 gives the output, then ...

A) if the input is 8, what is the output? _____

B) if the input is -9, what is the output? _____

C) if the output is 22, what is the input? _____

Name: _____ Date: _____

Chapter 7: Using Algebra to Generalize Patterns (cont.)

5. For the input/output table, find each of the following:

Input	Output
1	0
3	4
-2	-6
-4	-10
0	-2

A) If the input is -5, what is the output? _____

B) If 86 is the output, what is the input? _____

C) Describe the rule in words: _____

_____

D) Describe the rule in symbols: if n is the input, _____

6. The first five terms in the sequence, 52, 50, 48, 46, 44, …, have been entered into an input/output table.

Input	Output
1	52
2	50
3	48
4	46
5	44

A) If the input is 20, what is the output? _____

B) If 4 is the output, what is the input? _____

C) Describe the rule in words: _____

_____

D) Describe the rule in symbols: if n is the input, _____

E) If -3 could be considered an input, what would you think the output would be?

_____

Name: _____   Date: _____

Chapter 7: Using Algebra to Generalize Patterns (cont.)

7. The first five terms in the sequence, 13, 17, 21, 25, 29, …. have been entered into an input/output table.

Input	Output
1	13
2	17
3	21
4	25
5	29

A) If the input is 20, what is the output? _____

B) If 425 is the output, what is the input? _____

C) Describe the rule in words: _____

_____

D) Describe the rule in symbols: if n is the input, _____

E) If -3 could be considered an input, what would you think the output would be?

_____

8. If an input/output table was made with the following rule: subtracting seven from eight times the input equals the output, then ...

A) if the input is 10, what is the output? _____

B) if the output is 33, what is the input? _____

C) describe the rule in symbols: if n is the input, _____

9. If an input/output table was made with the following rule: adding three to the input, multiplying by seven, and subtracting 2 gives the output, then ...

A) if the input is 10, what is the output? _____

B) if the output is 61, what is the input? _____

C) describe the rule in symbols: if n is the input,

_____

Name: _____   Date: _____

Chapter 7: Using Algebra to Generalize Patterns (cont.)

10. If an input/output table was made with the following rule: subtract one from the input, square that, and add 9 equals the output, then ...

A) if the input is 10, what is the output? _____

B) if the output is 58, what is the input? _____

C) describe the rule in symbols: if *n* is the input, _____

Challenge Problems: Generalizing Patterns in Tables

1. For the input/output table, find each of the following:

Input	Output
1	5
3	9
-2	-1
-4	-5
0	3

A) If the input is -5, what is the output? _____

B) If 23 is the output, what is the input? _____

C) Describe the rule in words: _____

_____

D) Describe the rule in symbols: if *n* is the input, _____

2. Complete an input/output table for the following rule given in words: add two to the input, triple that, and then add five more than the input.

Input	Output
1	
5	
-2	
-4	
0	

A) If the input is -5, what is the output? _____

B) If 23 is the output, what is the input? _____

C) Describe the rule in symbols: if *n* is the input,

_____

Chapter 7: Using Algebra to Generalize Patterns (cont.)

3. For the input/output table, find each of the following:

Input	Output
1	16
3	36
-2	1
-4	1
0	9

A) If the input is -5, what is the output? _____

B) If 81 is the output, what is the input? _____

C) Describe the rule in words: _____

_____

D) Describe the rule in symbols: if n is the input,

_____

4. Complete an input/output table for the following rule given in words: subtract one from the input, square that, and then add one, and subtract the input.

Input	Output
1	
5	
-2	
-4	
0	

A) If the input is -5, what is the output? _____

B) If 30 is the output, what is the input? _____

C) Describe the rule in symbols: if n is the input, _____

Name: _____ Date: _____

Chapter 7: Using Algebra to Generalize Patterns (cont.)

Basic Overview: Generalizing Patterns in Algebraic Expressions and Equations

Being able to describe rules using symbols means that we are forming and working with algebraic expressions and equations. An algebraic expression is a combination of numbers, variables, and operations. In other words, it consists of terms that are combined using addition, subtraction, multiplication, or division. To have an equation, an equal sign is used to show how two algebraic expressions are related.

Example of Generalizing Patterns in Algebraic Expressions and Equations:

Translate into symbols: the number of chairs needed is twice the number of tables.

We can use symbols (*c* for chairs and *t* for tables) and translate the situation into an equation,

$c = 2t$

Practice: Generalizing Patterns in Algebraic Expressions and Equations

Directions: Translate each into an algebraic expression or equation. Label each answer as EXP(expression) or EQ(equation).

1. Seven less than the square of a number _____

2. Six more than three times the number _____

3. The sum of twice a number and seven is fifteen. _____

4. Ten more than twice the number of people invited _____

5. Twelve subtracted from half a number is eight. _____

6. Eighteen increased by twelve times a number is fifty. _____

7. Ten more than seven times a number _____

8. Fifteen is forty less than half the sum of the number and eight. _____

9. Twice a number decreased by a third of the number _____

Chapter 7: Using Algebra to Generalize Patterns (cont.)

10. Add ten to my age and double the result. _____

11. John starts Sunday with a certain amount of money in his pocket. For each succeeding day of one week, he increases his sum by that same amount plus an extra dollar for each day that has passed. _____

12. I had forty dollars left after spending half of my money and then losing $8.

_____

13. My grade on the first test plus 40 was the same as half my grade on the first test plus 60.

_____

14. I started with some money and gained $6 the first day. For the next two days, I gained $6 more than I gained the previous day and ended up with $120.

_____

15. I had some money, and I gave away ten dollars the first day, gained three times my original amount the second day, and noticed that I now had $80.

_____

Challenge Problems: Generalizing Patterns in Algebraic Expressions and Equations

Directions: Write an equation or expression for each word problem.

1. A number added to fifty is the same as subtracting the number from ten.

_____

2. Twice a number decreased by a third of the number is the same as the number decreased by nine. _____

3. Add ten to my age and double the result, and you get the same value if you triple my age and subtract 5. _____

4. John starts Sunday with a certain amount of money in his pocket. For each succeeding day of one week, he increases his sum by that same amount plus an extra dollar for each day that has passed. At the end of the week, his total is five times the amount of money that he added on Saturday. _____

Name: _____ Date: _____

Chapter 7: Using Algebra to Generalize Patterns (cont.)

Basic Overview: Solving Simple Linear Equations

A linear equation can have number terms and variable terms—but the variable is raised only to the first power—so no squares or roots or any other exponents can be present. Linear equations will have only one solution. Solving linear equations is simply a matter of keeping the balance in the equation—and using what you know about inverses.

Equal Addition Rule

To undo addition, subtract the same amount from both sides. To undo subtraction, add the same amount to both sides. The new equation is equivalent to the original.

Equal Multiplication Rule

To undo multiplication, divide by the same amount on both sides of the equation. To undo division, multiply by the same amount on both sides. The new equation is equivalent to the original equation.

Example of the Equal Addition Rule:

$6y + 7 = 9y - 4$
$-6y + 6y + 7 = -6y + 9y - 4$
$7 = 3y - 4$
$7 + 4 = 3y - 4 + 4$
$11 = 3y$

Example of Solving a Linear Equation:

$x + 6 = 15$
$x + 6 - 6 = 15 - 6$
$x = 9$ (since $6 - 6 = 0$ and $15 - 6 = 9$)

Example of the Equal Multiplication Rule:

$-5y = 25$

$$\frac{-5y}{-5} = \frac{25}{-5}$$

$y = -5$

Name: _____   Date: _____

Chapter 7: Using Algebra to Generalize Patterns (cont.)

PART 1

Practice: Using Algebra to Generalize Patterns Solving Linear Equations

Directions: Solve each linear equation.

1. $-6x = 36$ _____

2. $a + 8 = 37$ _____

3. $23 = 2 + 3x$ _____

4. $2x + 10 = -26$ _____

5. $b + 7 + 2b = 28$ _____

6. $-5x = 35$ _____

7. $a + 5 = 37$ _____

8. $23 = 1 + 2x$ _____

9. $4x + 10 = -26$ _____

10. $5b + 7 + 2b = 23$ _____

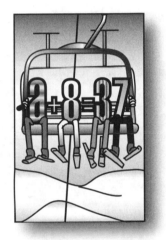

Challenge Problems: Using Algebra to Generalize Patterns Solving Linear Equations

Directions: Solve each linear equation.

1. $6x - 9 = 6x + 12$ _____

2. $3x - a = 12$ has a solution of $x = 5$. What is the value of a? _____

3. $3(x - 5) + 2 = 7 - x$ _____

4. $6x - 5 = 12x + 5$ _____

5. $3(4 - x) = 5(2x - 9)$ _____

Name: _____ Date: _____

Chapter 7: Using Algebra to Generalize Patterns (cont.)

PART 2

Practice: Using Algebra to Generalize Patterns Solving Linear Equations

Directions: Solve each linear equation.

1. $-3x = 42$ _____

2. $m - 5 = 12$ _____

3. $7 = 5 - 2x$ _____

4. $3x - 10 = 5$ _____

5. $4b - 7 + b = 23$ _____

6. $2(x + 1) = 20$ _____

7. $5x - 19 = 11$ _____

8. $9 - 4x = 18$ _____

9. $18 - 5x = 4x$ _____

10. $3x + 5x - 18x = 83$ _____

11. $4(2 - x) = 11 - 2x$ _____

12. $3 + 7x = -2x + 21$ _____

13. $4x - 2(1 - x) = 28$ _____

14. $4x - 2(1 + x) = 28$ _____

15. $3(2x - 3) = (1 - 3x)2$ _____

16. $210x = 2.1$ _____

17. $2.1x = 210$ _____

18. $0.3(x - 2) = 5$ _____

19. $5.2(3 + 2x) = 14$ _____

20. If $3.1x + b = b$, what is the value for x?

_____

Chapter 7: Using Algebra to Generalize Patterns (cont.)

Checking Progress: Using Algebra to Generalize Patterns

1. A) Fill in the next numbers in the sequence: 17, 23, 29, 35, 41, _____, _____, _____, ...

    B) What is the 15th term? _____

2. What is the 62nd term in the sequence? 87, 84, 81, 78, ... _____

3. The terms for one sequence are given by $11 + 4x$, while the terms in another sequence are given by $53 - 3x$. Will the sequences ever have the same value for a given term number?

    _____

4. For the input/output table, find each of the following:

Input	Output
1	6
3	16
-2	-9
-4	-19
0	1

    A) If the input is -5, what is the output? _____

    B) If 46 is the output, what is the input? _____

    C) Describe the rule in words: _____

    _____

    D) Describe the rule in symbols: if n is the input, _____

5. If an input/output table was made with the following rule, one-half the input subtracted from two more than the input gives the output, then ...

    A) if the input is 10, what is the output? _____

    B) if the output is 0, what is the input? _____

    C) describe the rule in symbols: if n is the input, _____

Name: _____ Date: _____

Chapter 7: Using Algebra to Generalize Patterns (cont.)

6. The first five terms in the sequence, -3, -1, 1, 3, 5, , ..., have been entered into an input/output table.

Input	Output
1	-3
2	-1
3	1
4	3
5	5

A) If the input is 20, what is the output? _____

B) If 91 is the output, what is the input? _____

C) Describe the rule in words: _____

_____

D) Describe the rule in symbols: if *n* is the input, _____

E) If -3 could be considered an input, what do you think the output would be?

_____

7. Write the following equation with variables: twice the sum of a number and seven is

fifteen. _____

8. Write the following expression with variables: a number decreased by one more than

half the number. _____

9. Solve for *a*: 13*a* – 7 – 3*a* = 23 _____

10. Solve for *x*: 2(3*x* – 5) = (1 + 4*x*)2 _____

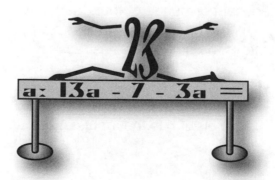

Name: _____ Date: _____

Chapter 8: Problem-Solving Strategies

Basic Overview: Problem Solving With Tables

When trying to solve a problem, it helps to have a systematic plan. One way of solving problems is to use models. Other strategies include making a table; guess, check and revise; and writing equations. George Polya was a mathematician who devised a four-step plan for problem solving.

1. Understand the problem.
2. Devise a plan—Choose a strategy.
3. Carry out the plan—Put the strategy to work.
4. Look back.

Example of Problem Solving With a Table:

1. **Understand the problem.**

   Mario is the pitcher for the local minor league baseball team. He has figured out that his salary breaks down to $1,000 per game plus $50 per pitch. If Mario was paid $6,250 for his last game, how many pitches did he throw in that game?

Identify what is known.	Salary is $1,000. Bonus of $50 per pitch Total salary was $6,250.
What do we want to know?	How many pitches did he throw?

2. **Devise a plan, and**
3. **Carry out the plan.**

   For this problem, any one of four strategies could work. We could make a table; use the guess, check, and revise strategy; draw a diagram; or create and solve a linear equation. We will demonstrate making a table in this section, and later in the chapter, we will create and solve a linear equation.

Make a Table Strategy

# of Pitches	15	30	45	60	75	90	105
Salary Bonus	$1,000 + 50(15)	$1,000 + 50(30)	$1,000 + 50(45)	$1,000 + 50(60)	$1,000 + 50(75)	$1,000 + 50(90)	$1,000 + 50(105)
Total	= $1,750	= $2,500	= $3,250	= $4,000	= $4,750	= $5,500	= $6,250

75

Chapter 8: Problem-Solving Strategies (cont.)

In filling out the table, the bonus costs rise by $50 for each pitch. In order to make the table a manageable size, increments of 15 pitches are used. By following the pattern, the salary of $6,250 is reached when the input of 105 pitches is used.

Note that your table could have had entries by 2s or inputs by 5s—different choices would mean fewer or more trials to find the answer needed.

4. Look back.

The solution of 105 pitches checks out for a salary of $6,250. Have we answered the question? Yes. We wanted to know how many pitches Mario made to receive a salary of $6,250.

Mario made 105 pitches.

Practice: Problem Solving With Tables

Directions: On your own paper, create a table to answer each of the following questions. Write your final answers on the blanks provided.

1. Dan has $10 less than Chris. Together they have $80. How much money does each one have?

   _____

2. The concession stand sold three types of drinks. One evening they sold half as many sports drinks as they did cola and three times as many bottles of water as sports drinks. A total of 600 drinks was sold. How many bottles of each type of drink were sold?

   _____

3. Matemica bacteria divide every 15 minutes. If you start with one matemica bacterium, how many bacteria will be present in 3 hours?

   _____

4. What is the area of a square that has a perimeter of 52 meters?

   _____

Name: _____ Date: _____

Chapter 8: Problem-Solving Strategies (cont.)

5. Stefano started college with $5,000 in savings and spent $150 per month. During the same time, Neelie started college with $200 and was able to save $150 per month. When did Stefano and Neelie have the same amount of money in savings?

_____

6. Katie liked to pose puzzles to her grandchildren, Andrea and Brian, who are 14 and 11 years old, respectively. One day, the grandchildren asked Katie how old she was. Katie said, "If you take one-half of my age and subtract Brian's age from that, you will get the same result as adding five less than Andrea's age to one-fourth of my age." How old was Katie?

_____

7. If one-third of a number plus one-half of a number is 60, what is the number?

_____

8. If I triple the amount of money I have and gain another seven dollars, I will have the exact amount needed to pay for the $55 ticket to attend the concert. How much money do I now have?

_____

9. Three added to twice a number gives the same result as 7 added to the number. What is the number?

_____

10. When I asked what score I received on the test, Ms. Nowit Ahl told me the following: if you triple your score and subtract 9, you will get the same result if you double your score and add 82.

_____

Name: _____ Date: _____

Chapter 8: Problem-Solving Strategies (cont.)

Basic Overview: Problem Solving With Linear Equations

One of the major goals of algebra is to solve problems. In solving problems, many times there are several strategies or approaches that can be used to find the solution. The strategies of (1) Make a table; (2) Guess, check and revise; and (3) Draw a diagram may be approaches that will work to solve a linear problem, but algebra allows us to use variables and add the strategy, (4) Write an equation, to our problem-solving toolkit. In solving many problems, an equation or formula is helpful and the most efficient route to a solution. An equation allows us to describe the relationship between two or more quantities. While there are many types of equations that can be identified and learned in an algebra course, the vast majority of situations involving modeling with equations require the use of linear equations.

Example of Problem Solving With a Linear Equation:

Mario is the pitcher for the local minor league baseball team. He has figured out that his salary breaks down to $1,000 per game plus $50 per pitch. If Mario was paid $6,250 for his last game, how many pitches did he throw in that game?

Let x represent the number of pitches.
Then, his salary is $1,000 plus $50 per pitch should equal the total salary, $6,250.
Translate that into an equation: $1{,}000 + 50x = 6{,}250$.

Solve the equation.

- We want to find the value of x that makes the equation work. We want to isolate x by itself, or as we sometimes say, solve for x.

- Consider the equation. What is the first thing in the way of getting x by itself? The 1,000. How do we undo addition? Subtract! Just be sure to keep the balance by subtracting the same amount from each side of the equation.

$$\begin{array}{r} 1{,}000 + 50x = 6{,}250 \\ \underline{-1{,}000 \qquad\quad -1{,}000} \\ 50x = 5{,}250 \end{array}$$

- What do you need to do next to find out what the value of x is? The only thing left is the 50 being multiplied by x. How do you undo multiplication? Divide! Just be sure to keep the balance of the equation by dividing both sides by the same amount.

Name: _____ Date: _____

Chapter 8: Problem-Solving Strategies (cont.)

$50x = 5,250$

$$\frac{50x}{50} = \frac{5,250}{50}$$

$x = 105$

- Check your work by using the answer. If Mario made 105 pitches, his salary is:

$1,000 + $50(105) = $1,000 + $5,250 = $6,250

- Have we answered the question, "How many pitches did he throw?" ? Yes.

Mario threw 105 pitches in the game.

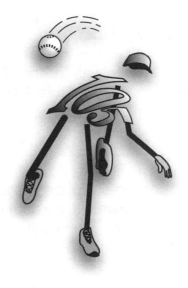

Name: _____ Date: _____

Chapter 8: Problem-Solving Strategies (cont.)

Practice: Using Linear Equations to Solve Problems

Directions: Write an equation and solve the equation to find the answer for each problem.

1. A board is 24 feet long. It is sawed into 2 pieces. One piece is 0.5 feet longer than the other. How many feet long is each piece?

   _____

2. Tyrone had one-fourth as many books as Lei. Together they have 60 books. How many books does each have?

   _____

3. There are 12 people on a jury. Six more jurors voted to convict than voted not to convict the person on trial. How many voted to convict?

   _____

4. Laticia had 16 fewer pencils than Kim. They had a total of 40 pencils. How many pencils did each have?

   _____

5. Sivart and Brab were writing test questions for the Niawt Publishing Company. They wrote 400 questions between them. If Brab wrote 20 questions more than Sivart, how many questions did each write?

   _____

6. Elaine and Skyler loved to travel, especially to sports stadiums in the summer. At the end of one summer, they compared their travels. They determined that they visited stadiums a total of 79 times and that Elaine visited five less than three times the number of visits Skyler made. How many visits to stadiums did each make?

   _____

7. A softball team won 2 more than three times as many games as it lost. It won 86 games. How many did it lose?

   _____

Name: _____ Date: _____

Chapter 8: Problem-Solving Strategies (cont.)

8.) Dividing a number by 2 yields the same result as subtracting 15 from three times the number. What is the number?

_____

9.) A purchase of 20 stamps, some costing $0.34 and some costing $0.27, totaled $6.45. How many of each stamp was purchased?

_____

10.) A company has 5 large buses and 6 smaller ones. A large bus holds 11 more people than the smaller one. If the capacity of all the buses is 495, how much does each size of bus hold?

_____

Challenge Problems: Problem Solving

Directions: Use the problem-solving strategies you have learned to solve the problems. There is more than one way to solve each. Use your own paper if you need more room.

1.) Sneab Gas Company charges a base rate plus $12.25 per M.C.F. of gas used per month. If Noslo's gas bill for a month was $137.50 and included 10 M. C. F.'s of gas, what is the base rate charged by Sneab Gas Company?

_____

2.) Yolanda had her cell phone plan with Berison. Her plan cost $78 per month for 550 minutes with a per-minute charge of $0.40 for any minutes over 550. One month, Yolanda had a bill from Berison for $98. How many extra minutes did Yolanda use that month?

_____

3.) Make a table: Einstein Elementary School used recycling efforts to raise money for textbooks. Each plastic bottle they recycled was worth 5¢, and each pound of paper was worth 2¢. One week they raised $20. What are some possible values for the pounds of paper and number of bottles they recycled?

_____

Name: _____ Date: _____

Chapter 8: Problem-Solving Strategies (cont.)

Directions: Write an equation and solve the problem.

4. The winner in an election won by a ratio of 4 to 3. If the winner received 4,520 votes, how many votes were cast in the election?

_____

5. Papa Noj's Pizza is offering a special. It has a base price for the pizza special plus $1.75 for each additional item. Ryan loves pizza and purchased the special. He paid $17.45 for his pizza, which had six additional items. What was the base price for the pizza?

_____

6. For Mother's Day, Chad bought 12 scarves; for Father's Day, Chad bought 2 ties. If a tie costs $8 more than two scarves, how much did each item cost if Chad paid a total of $112?

_____

Checking Progress: Problem-Solving Strategies

Directions: Use the problem-solving strategies you have learned to solve the following problems. You may want to write an equation and solve it to find the answer for each problem, but there may be more than one way to solve each problem.

1. Rip-Off Plumbing charges a flat rate for a house call, plus an amount per hour. If the flat rate is $f and the per-hour charge is $37.50, what is the expression that represents the total charge for a visit by Rip-Off Plumbing for a visit of h hours? Mr. Sanchez had a bill from Rip-Off Plumbing for $95 for a two-hour visit. What is the flat rate charged by Rip-Off Plumbing?

_____

2. Selena and Peyton were writing test questions for the Niawt Publishing Company. They wrote 400 questions between them. If Peyton would have written 30 more questions, she would have written the same amount as Selena. How many questions did each write?

_____

Name: _____ Date: _____

Chapter 8: Problem-Solving Strategies (cont.)

3. Katie likes to pose puzzles to her grandchildren, Andrea and Brian, who are 14 and 11 years old, respectively. One day the grandchildren asked Katie how old Grandpa was. Katie said, "If you take one-half of Grandpa's age and add nine less than twice Brian's age, you will get Grandpa's age minus twice Andrea's age." How old was Grandpa?

_____

4. The winner in an election won by a ratio of 4 to 3. If there were 4,550 votes cast in the election, how many votes did the winner receive?

_____

5. Fodgather's Pizza is offering a special. It has a base price of $5.55 for the pizza plus a fixed cost per each additional item. Kimiko loves pizza and purchased the special. She paid $13.95 for her pizza that had six additional items. What was the cost for each additional topping?

_____

6. Elaine and Skyler like refreshments, especially ice cream and pizza, when visiting amusement parks. Over the summer, they found that they purchased ice cream and pizza a total of 873 times, and that they purchased ice cream twelve more than twice the number of times they purchased pizza. How many purchases of ice cream and pizza did they make over the summer?

_____

7. When I asked what score I received on the test, Ms. Nowit Ahl told me the following: if you quadruple your score and subtract 9, you will get the same result as if you triple your score and add 82.

_____

8. The Crystal Falls School District has 8 large buses and 2 smaller ones. A small bus holds 8 more people than half the larger one. If the capacity of all the buses is 556, how much does each size of bus hold?

_____

Check-Up Problems: Real Numbers

Directions: Using the words listed below, fill in the blanks with the correct number type(s).

Real Number	Rational Number	Integer	Whole Number	Irrational Number

Number   **Type or Types**

1. 0.3232323232   _____

2. 44 ÷ 11   _____

3. $\sqrt{\sqrt{121}}$ _____

4. -3.2   _____

5. $1.3\overline{13}$ _____

6. $\dfrac{52}{1.3}$ _____

7. 5.111111…   _____

8. $\dfrac{5\pi}{3\pi}$ _____

9. $\dfrac{15\pi}{3}$ _____

10. $\sqrt{-4}$ _____

Name: _____ Date: _____

Check-Up Problems: Operations of Numbers and Variables

Directions: Perform the indicated operations.

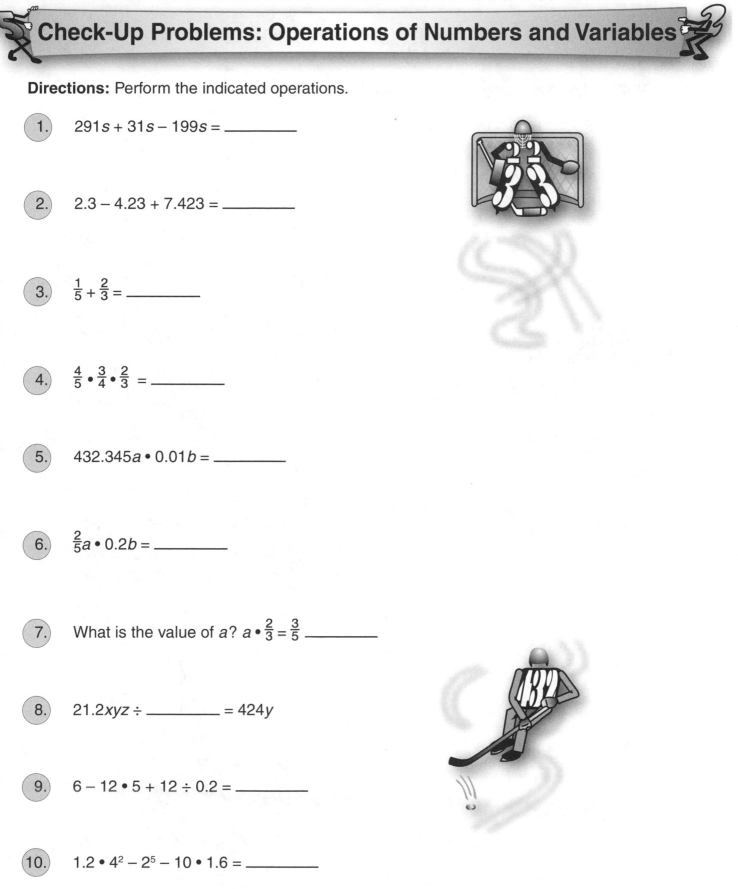

1. $291s + 31s - 199s = $ _____

2. $2.3 - 4.23 + 7.423 = $ _____

3. $\frac{1}{5} + \frac{2}{3} = $ _____

4. $\frac{4}{5} \cdot \frac{3}{4} \cdot \frac{2}{3} = $ _____

5. $432.345a \cdot 0.01b = $ _____

6. $\frac{2}{5}a \cdot 0.2b = $ _____

7. What is the value of a? $a \cdot \frac{2}{3} = \frac{3}{5}$ _____

8. $21.2xyz \div$ _____ $= 424y$

9. $6 - 12 \cdot 5 + 12 \div 0.2 = $ _____

10. $1.2 \cdot 4^2 - 2^5 - 10 \cdot 1.6 = $ _____

Name: _____ Date: _____

Check-Up Problems: Integers

Directions: Solve the following problems involving integers.

1.) $10 - 19 - 18 + 17 + 16 - 5 + 2 - 1 =$ _____

2.) $-10 - (-90) - (-8) + (-70) + (-6) - (-5) + (-2) - (-1) =$ _____

3.) $100 + 90 - 80 - 70 + 60 - 50 - 40 - 30 + 20 + 10 =$ _____

4.) $199 - 232 =$ _____ $- (-305)$

5.) _____ $+ (-305) = 48,934 + 305$

6.) $[-24 \cdot (-5)] + (-24 \cdot 12) + [-24 \cdot (-7)] =$ _____

7.) $(-24 \cdot 15) - (-24 \cdot 12) = 24 \cdot$ _____

8.) $(43 \div 5) - ($ _____ $\div 5) = 5$

9.) $-44 \div$ _____ $= 44 \div (-11)$

10.) $-5 \cdot |8 - 12 - 3 - 9| =$ _____

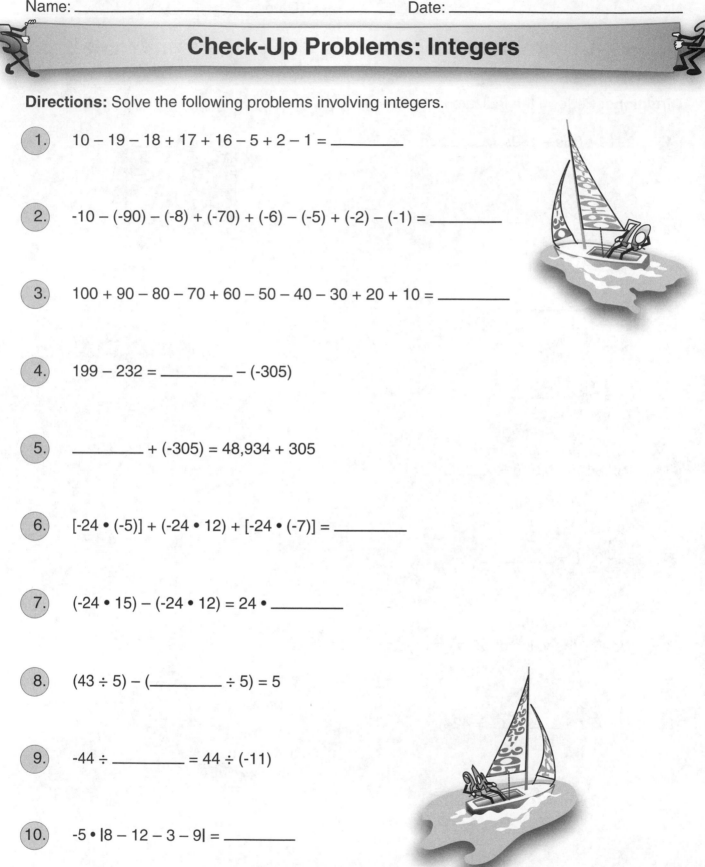

Name: _____ Date: _____

Check-Up Problems: Properties

Directions: Use a property of real numbers to generate a solution to each problem.

1. $392 + (-5{,}166) + (-62) + 1{,}282 + (-392) + (-1{,}282) + 5{,}166 =$ _____

2. _____ $+ 99 \cdot 861 = 99 \cdot 861 + 122$

3. $33a + 219b \cdot 421z =$ _____ $\cdot 421z + 33a$

4. $329a + ($ _____ $+$ _____ $) = (329a + 290z) + 413a$

5. Use the Associative Property of Addition to mentally compute the following.
   $(287 + 881) + 119$

   _____

6. Explain how to mentally compute the following by using the Associative Property of Multiplication. $(923{,}234 \cdot 2) \cdot 5$

   _____

7. Mentally simplify using the Distributive Property. $(13 \cdot 15) + (13 \cdot 5)$

   _____

8. $(3a \cdot 31b) + (3a \cdot 14c) = 3a \cdot ($ _____ $+$ _____ $)$

9. Rewrite using the Distributive Property. $43b^8 + 19b^5$

   _____

10. Which property is illustrated by the following? $\frac{5}{17} \cdot (314 + 95) = \frac{5}{17} \cdot (95 + 314)$

    _____

Name: _____   Date: _____

Check-Up Problems: Exponents and Exponential Expressions

Directions: Complete the following.

1. Evaluate. 0.03^3 _____

2. Evaluate. -5^3 _____

3. What is the largest integer value for b so that $3^b < 2{,}000$?

   _____

4. Evaluate. $12^2 \cdot 100$ _____

5. Evaluate. $-(2 \cdot -3)^3$ _____

6. Combine terms. $4a^2 - (33b^4 - 17a^2) - 34b^4$ _____

7. Combine terms. $4a^2 - [(33b^4 - 17a^2) - 34b^4]$ _____

8. Combine terms. $a^4 \cdot b^9 \cdot b^{13} \cdot a^{41} \cdot b^5$ _____

9. Rewrite 3^{-3} using only positive exponents. The value is _____.

10. Combine terms. $((y^{12})^2)^5$ _____

11. Write the following in scientific notation. $77.8 \cdot 13.2$ _____

12. Find the value of t. $0.00000088888 \cdot 10^t = 0.00088888$ _____

Name: _____ Date: _____

Check-Up Problems: Square Roots

Directions: Simplify each expression. Remember, a radical is not simplified if it has a radical in the denominator.

1. $\sqrt{(81)(36)}$ _____

2. $\sqrt{841}$ _____

3. $\sqrt{121z^{12}}$ _____

4. $(a^2\sqrt{az^9})(z\sqrt{z^{14}a^5})$, $a > 0$, $z > 0$ _____

5. $\sqrt{2^9 11^5 13^2}$ _____

6. $(\sqrt{48})(\sqrt{15})$ _____

7. $\dfrac{\sqrt{99}}{\sqrt{45}}$ _____

8. $\left(\dfrac{\sqrt{84}}{\sqrt{44}}\right)\left(\dfrac{\sqrt{55}}{\sqrt{35}}\right)$ _____

9. $z\sqrt{2z} - 2\sqrt{8z}$ _____

10. $3\sqrt{6z^5} + 5\sqrt{24z^3}$ _____

Name: _____ Date: _____

Check-Up Problems: Using Algebra to Generalize Patterns

Directions: Complete the following problems.

1. A) Fill in the next numbers in the sequence: -5, -1, 3, 7, 11, _____, _____, _____, …

    B) What is the 15th term? _____

2. What is the 62nd term in the sequence? 13, 33, 53, 73, … _____

3. The terms for one sequence are given by $8 + 5x$, while the terms in another sequence are given by $50 - 2x$. Will the sequences ever have the same value for a given term number? _____

4. For the input/output table, find each of the following:

Input	Output
1	6
3	12
-2	-3
-4	-9
0	3

    A) If the input is -5, what is the output? _____

    B) If 123 is the output, what is the input? _____

    C) Describe the rule in words: _____

    _____

    D) Describe the rule in symbols: if n is the input, _____

5. If an input/output table was made with the following rule, one-half the input added to 14 gives the output, then …

    A) if the input is 10, what is the output? _____

    B) if the output is 0, what is the input? _____

    C) describe the rule in symbols: if n is the input, _____

Name: _____   Date: _____

Check-Up Problems: Using Algebra to Generalize Patterns (cont.)

6. The first five terms in the sequence, 24, 21, 18, 15, 12, …, have been entered into an input/output table.

Input	Output
1	24
2	21
3	18
4	15
5	12

A) If the input is 20, what is the output? _____

B) If -24 is the output, what is the input? _____

C) Describe the rule in words: _____

_____

D) Describe the rule in symbols: if n is the input, _____

E) If -3 could be considered an input, what do you think the output would be? _____

7. Write the following equation with variables: twice the sum of a number and eight subtracted from forty-two is sixteen.

_____

8. Write the following expression with variables: three times the sum of a number and nine decreased by six.

_____

9. Solve for b. $-5 + b = 23 - (4b - 7)$ _____

10. Solve for x. $4(2x - 3) = (3 - 2x)2$ _____

Name: _____ Date: _____

Check-Up Problems: Problem-Solving Strategies

Directions: Solve the following problems by using the problem-solving strategies you have learned.

1. The length of one side of a rectangle is 24 yards more than the width. If the perimeter of the rectangle is 120 yards, what are the lengths of the sides of the rectangle?

_____

2. Land Send sells clothing over the Internet. Imin Styl ordered six shirts, each of which cost the same amount. Land Send's charge for shipping and handling is $8.95 per order. What expression gives the value of the total amount Imin will be charged for the order? If his total cost is $158.95, what was the cost of each shirt?

_____

3. Bosnak was designing a house with a rectangular floor plan. The original design had the length twice the width. He changed the plan by adding 3' to each dimension. The total perimeter of the new design is now 186'. What are the dimensions of the new floor design?

_____

4. The winner in an election won by a ratio of 4 to 3. If the loser received 4,521 votes, how many votes were cast in the election?

_____

5. Anat and Evad are both avid bike riders, but each lives in a different town. One day they made an arrangement to bike toward each other and camp where they met. Their towns were 100 miles apart, and they started riding at the same time. Anat rode her bike at 11 miles per hour, while Evad rode his bike at 14 miles per hour. How far were they from Anat's town when they met?

_____

Check-Up Problems: Problem-Solving Strategies (cont.)

6. Katie likes to pose puzzles for her grandchildren, Andrea and Brian, who are 14 and 11 years old, respectively. One day, the grandchildren asked Katie how long she and Grandpa had been married. Katie said, "If you add Andrea's age to one-third of the years we have been married, you will get the same result as adding one more than the difference between Andrea's and Brian's ages to one-half the years we have been married." How long have Grandpa and Grandma been married?

_____

7. Snakey's Pizza is offering a special. It has a base price for the pizza special plus $1.35 per each additional item. Su loves pizza and purchased the special. She paid $13.45 for her pizza, which had six additional items. What was the base price for the pizza?

_____

8. Elaine and Skyler especially like Twister Ride and Haunted House Ride when they visit amusement parks. During the summer, they determined that they had ridden the two rides 397 times. They rode Twister thirteen more than one-third the amount of times they went on the Haunted House ride. How many times did they ride each?

_____

9. When I asked what score I received on my test, Ms. Nowit Ahl told me the following: if you multiply your score by five and subtract 9, you will get the same result as if you quadruple your score and add 82.

_____

10. A company has 3 large buses and 9 smaller ones. A large bus holds 5 more people than twice the smaller one. If the capacity of all the buses is 255, how much does each size of bus hold?

_____

Practice Answer Keys

Chapter 1: Practice: Which Number Is Which? (p. 6)

1. Real, Rational, Integer, Whole
2. Real, Rational, Integer
3. Real, Rational
4. Real, Rational
5. Real, Rational
6. Real, Rational, Integer, Whole
7. Real, Rational
8. Real, Rational, Integer, Whole
9. Real, Rational
10. Real, Irrational
11. Real, Rational
12. Real, Irrational
13. Real, Rational, Integer
14. Real, Rational, Integer, Whole
15. Real, Rational
16. Real, Irrational
17. Real, Rational, Integer
18. Real, Rational
19. Real, Rational, Integer, Whole [This is based on the fact that 3.2 + 4.8 = 8]
20. Cannot be determined

Chapter 1: Challenge Problems: Real Numbers (p. 7)

1. Real, Rational, Integer, Whole Number (even though there is a negative sign with it, the value of this number is 0, which is a whole number)
2. Real, Rational, Integer, Whole Number, Natural. This is not an irrational number. While there is a radical sign, $\sqrt{4}$ is the same value as 2, and $4 \div 2 = 2$.
3. Real, Rational, Integer
4. None of these. [Because you cannot find a real number that when squared has the value of -4]
5. Real, Rational, Integer, Whole, Natural. This is another expression for the number 1. While this may seem puzzling, one way to think about it is like this. We know that $\frac{1}{3} + \frac{2}{3} = 1$. But $\frac{1}{3} + \frac{2}{3} = 0.333333\ldots + 0.6666666\ldots$. This is the same as $0.999999999\ldots$, which thus must be 1.
6. Irrational
7. Real, Rational
8. Real, Rational [This is because $\frac{2\pi}{5\pi}$ is equivalent to $\frac{2}{5}$.]
9. Real, Rational, Integer, Whole [This is because $1 - 2 + 3 - 4 + 5 = 3$.]
10. Real, Rational, Integer, Whole Number [This is because $4 \cdot 3.5 = 14$.]

Practice Answer Keys (cont.)

Chapter 1: Checking Progress: Real Numbers (p. 8)
1. Rational Number, Real Number
2. Irrational Number, Real Number
3. Whole Number, Integer, Rational Number, Real Number
4. Rational Number, Real Number
5. Irrational Number, Real Number
6. Rational Number, Real Number
7. Rational Number, Real Number
8. Integer, Real Number, Rational Number, Whole Number
9. Integer, Real Number, Rational Number, Whole Number
10. Real Number, Irrational Number

Chapter 2: Practice: Addition and Subtraction of Numbers and Variables (p. 9–10)
1. -4
2. $41s$
3. $1.8a + 4$
4. Cannot be combined
5. 1,110
6. $-9b + 19$ or $19 - 9b$
7. 435
8. $430s + 5y$
9. $-365s$
10. $-435s$
11. $-435s$
12. 3,000
13. 184
14. 0
15. $5y - 5x$ [or $-5x + 5y$]
16. 1,111
17. $3,333a - 2,222b$
18. 13.953
19. $\frac{5}{6}$
20. Cannot be combined

Chapter 2: Challenge Problems: Addition and Subtraction of Numbers and Variables (p. 10)
1. 0
2. $-9z$
3. Cannot be combined
4. Wages: $562.50   Baseball cards: 15
5. There are multiple answers to this problem. Two of these are $3b + 2b + 100 + 1 - 130$; $8b + 3b - 6b + 10 + 19$.

Practice Answer Keys (cont.)

Chapter 2: Practice: Multiplication of Numbers and Variables (p. 11–12)

1. $\frac{2}{9}$
2. $\frac{120}{720}$ or $\frac{1}{6}$
3. $15ab$
4. 576
5. 0.432345
6. $4.32345ab$
7. $9.75st$
8. $20abc$
9. $20aaa$ or $20a^3$
10. $411ab$
11. $0.000001abc$
12. $4,900ab$
13. $18ab$
14. $\frac{1}{18}ab$
15. $0.2ab$
16. 48
17. 1
18. $7,000a$
19. Same (need explanations)
20. 7

Chapter 2: Challenge Problems: Multiplication of Numbers and Variables (p. 12)

1. $\frac{42}{12}b$, or $\frac{7}{2}b$, or $3.5b$
2. They have the same value.
3. $28b$
4. $42,512.35$
5. There are many answers to this question. Three are: let $x = 3a$ and $y = \frac{1}{2}bc$; let $x = abc$ and $y = \frac{3}{2}$; let $x = 30c$ and $y = \frac{1}{20}ab$.

Chapter 2: Practice: Dividision of Numbers and Variables (p. 13–14)

1. 4
2. 12
3. 42.5
4. $425,000$
5. $\dfrac{425,000a}{b}$

Practice Answer Keys (cont.)

6. $\dfrac{425,000a}{b}$ [While it looks different, this is the same problem as number 5.]

7. $\dfrac{9a}{b}$

8. $\dfrac{9}{5}$

9. These have the same value.

10. These have the same value.

11. 0

12. $\dfrac{14y}{3x}$

13. $\dfrac{xz}{2}$

14. $144xy^2z$

15. $\dfrac{y}{3x}$

16. $\dfrac{1}{3}$

17. 0

18. These are the same.

19. $\dfrac{12}{37} \div \dfrac{4}{31}$ has the larger value. $\dfrac{93}{37} > \dfrac{1}{3}$

20. 0.001

Chapter 2: Challenge Problems: Dividing Numbers and Variables (p. 14)

1. 71

2. This computation is not possible. Division by 0 is undefined.

3. There are many solutions. Four solutions are: $a = 25zy$ and $b = 6x$; $a = 50zy$ and $b = 12x$;

   $a = 25zyc$ and $b = 6xc$; $a = \dfrac{1}{6x}$ and $b = \dfrac{1}{25yz}$.

4. Brad might have thought he could do the problem like this. $88 \div 11 = 8$, and $48 \div 6 = 8$, and $8 - 8 = 0$. The solution, however, is 8 because $88 - 48 = 40$, $11 - 6 = 5$, and $40 \div 5 = 8$.

5. Yes, these expressions are equivalent.

Chapter 2: Practice: Order of Operations (p. 16–17)

1. 1

2. $\dfrac{3}{25}$

3. 3

4. 2

5. -0.5 or $-\dfrac{1}{2}$

Practice Answer Keys (cont.)

6. This cannot be computed because $2 - 2 = 0$, and division by zero is undefined.
7. -8
8. -5
9. 250
10. 4
11. 4
12. 9
13. $13a - 5$
14. -0.5
15. -2.5
16. 26.6
17. $\frac{8}{5}a^2 + 25$, or $1.6a^2 + 25$
18. $8z - 13$
19. 30 [Can you see the 3 • 10 in this expression?]
20. 11
21. 32
22. 0
23. 0
24. 180
25. 180. [Do you see this is the same as question 24?]
26. $\frac{1}{7}$ [If you worked these as decimals, you should have a close approximation of $\frac{1}{7}$.]
27. $46a$
28. $\dfrac{128}{a}$
29. $68a$
30. Cannot be performed. Denominator is zero, and division by zero is undefined.
31. 16 [Can you see this as 12 sixteens, minus one sixteen, minus 10 sixteens, leaving one sixteen?]
32. 50
33. -20
34. -2604
35. 120
36. -990
37. -1728
38. 76
39. 37
40. $9s + 37$

Practice Answer Keys (cont.)

Chapter 2: Challenge Problems: Order of Operations (p. 18)
1. $2 \cdot (5 - 3) + 8 = 12$
2. There are multiple solutions. One solution is $(20 - 5) \cdot 4 \div (-2 + 5) = 20$.
3. $-4^2 = -16$, while $(-4)^2 = 16$, so $(-4)^2$ is the larger.
4. 6
5. 24
6. Cannot be combined without knowing the value for a.

Chapter 2: Checking Progress: Operations of Numbers and Variables (p. 18)
1. $326w + 19v$
2. -0.893
3. $\frac{8}{15}$
4. $\frac{2}{6} = \frac{1}{3}$
5. $9.75st$
6. $0.08ab = \frac{2}{25}ab$
7. 10 times larger
8. $\frac{y}{3x}$
9. 29
10. undefined

Chapter 3: Practice: Addition and Subtraction of Integers (p. 20–21)
1. -9
2. 3,330
3. -23
4. -5
5. 5
6. 2
7. 888
8. -888
9. 0
10. 34
11. -5
12. 1
13. -1
14. 10
15. -138
16. 489,341
17. -392
18. 6,818

Practice Answer Keys (cont.)

19. 392
20. -909

Chapter 3: Challenge Problems: Addition and Subtraction of Integers (p. 21)
1. In addition to these five, there are many others: $a = -5$, $b = -12$; $a = -51$, $b = -58$; $a = -7$, $b = -14$; $a = -13$, $b = -20$; $a = -10$, $b = -17$
2. 43,526 − (-29,098,090)
3. 25
4. 55
5. 550
6. -18

Chapter 3: Practice: Multiplication and Division of Integers (p. 22–23)
1. 12
2. 23
3. -1
4. -90
5. -69
6. 217
7. -40
8. 24
9. -24
10. -240
11. If you apply the distributive property, you will see that this solution is the same as that of problem #10, -240.
12. -3
13. 13
14. 11
15. -50
16. -100
17. 11
18. 11
19. 26
20. -7

Chapter 3: Challenge Problems: Multiplication and Division of Integers (p. 23)
1. These five are among the choices: $a = -8$, $b = -18$; $a = -9$, $b = -16$; $a = -12$, $b = -12$; $a = -1$, $b = -144$; $a = -72$, $b = -2$.
2. -43,526 − (-29,098,090)
3. -250
4. 20
5. The two values are equal.

Practice Answer Keys (cont.)

Chapter 3: Checking Progress: All Integers (p. 24)

1. 5
2. -1
3. -63
4. -1,138
5. 88,731
6. $(-24 \cdot 14) = -336$
7. -7
8. -7
9. -5
10. 150

Chapter 4: Practice: Identity Properties of Addition and Multiplication (p. 26)

1. $\dfrac{1}{432}$

2. $\dfrac{1}{0.23}$ or $\dfrac{100}{23}$

3. 0.0001 or $\dfrac{1}{10,000}$

4. 2,343
5. 0
6. 0

7. $\dfrac{213}{147}$

8. $\dfrac{2}{7}$
9. $-2x + (-2y) + (-z)$, or other equivalent forms, such as, $-2x - 2y + (-z)$, $-2x - 2y - z$, $-2y + (-z) - 2x$, etc.

10. $\dfrac{4}{0.15}$ or $\dfrac{400}{15}$ or $\dfrac{80}{3}$

Chapter 4: Challenge Problems: Identity Properties of Addition and Multiplication (p. 26)

1. $\dfrac{1}{483 + 951 - 17}$ or $\dfrac{1}{1,372}$

2. Yasmine probably thought that because $0.33 + 0.67 = 1$. No, she is not right. Even though $0.33 + 0.67 = 1$ is a true statement, it does not show a multiplicative inverse relationship, nor does it show an additive inverse relationship.

Practice Answer Keys (cont.)

3. 37
4. 3.5
5. No solution. There is no number which when multiplied by 0 will produce 1.

Chapter 4: Practice: Commutative Properties of Addition and Multiplication (p. 27–28)

1. (123 + 223) = 346; commutative property of multiplication
2. (897 + 909) = 1806; commutative property of addition
3. 22; commutative property of addition
4. $a + b$; commutative property of addition
5. $(\frac{1}{5} \cdot 7)$; commutative property of addition
6. (98 + 83) = 181; commutative property of multiplication.
7. 19b; commutative property of addition
8. (37a + 49b), commutative property of multiplication
9. (3.2m + 53); commutative property of addition
10. (98 + 17b + 54 + 31 + 9); commutative property of addition

Chapter 4: Challenge Problems: Commutative Properties of Addition and Multiplication (p. 28)

1. This statement is true for any number that is substituted.
2. 87,263 $\cdot \frac{2}{7}$ is the larger. One way to think about it is to use the commutative property of multiplication. Remember, $\frac{1}{5} \cdot$ 87,263 = 87,263 $\cdot \frac{1}{5}$. But as $\frac{2}{7}$ is larger than $\frac{1}{5}$, then 87,263 $\cdot \frac{2}{7}$ is larger than 87,263 $\cdot \frac{1}{5}$.
3. There are many solutions. One possible solution is: (3 + 2) $\cdot$ 5 = (2 + 3) $\cdot$ 5. Note that 5 is used twice and 4 is not used. That is okay! Another solution is (4 + 5) $\cdot$ 3 = (5 + 4) $\cdot$ 3.
4. There are many solutions. One possible solution is: (3 + 2) $\cdot$ 5 = 5 $\cdot$ (3 + 2). Another solution is (5 + 1) $\cdot$ 4 = 4 $\cdot$ (5 + 1).
5. There are two solutions. ((4s + 3n) $\cdot$ (9a + 2)) $\cdot$ 3 and 3 $\cdot$ ((9a + 2) $\cdot$ (4s + 3n)).

Chapter 4: Practice: Associative Properties of Addition and Multiplication (p. 29–30)

1. 29; associative property of multiplication
2. 5y; associative property of addition
3. 29z + 13a; associative property of addition
4. 3s; associative property of addition
5. 8g; associative property of multiplication
6. s; associative property of multiplication
7. (34 $\cdot$ 3) $\cdot$ 55,435; 2 $\cdot$ (49 $\cdot$ 55,435) = (2 $\cdot$ 49) $\cdot$ 55,435, and 34 $\cdot$ 3 = 102 while 2 $\cdot$ 49 = 98.
8. $(\frac{37}{59} \cdot \frac{2}{7}) \cdot$ 3.5 = $\frac{37}{59} \cdot (\frac{2}{7} \cdot$ 3.5). However, another name for 3.5 is $\frac{7}{2}$, and $\frac{2}{7} \cdot \frac{7}{2}$ = 1, so the solution is $\frac{37}{59}$.

Practice Answer Keys (cont.)

9. No. While the computation is correct, the associative property was not shown to have been used.
10. $(87 + 981) + 19 = 87 + (981 + 19) = 87 + 1{,}000 = 1{,}087$

Chapter 4: Challenge Problems: Associative Properties of Addition and Multiplication (p. 30)

1. There are multiple solutions. One solution is $(3 + 5) \bullet 4 \bullet 2 = ((3 + 5) \bullet 4) \bullet 2$.
2. Disagree. This demonstrates the commutative property of addition.
3. $5 \bullet (((3 + 4) + 7) \bullet 9)$ using the associate property of multiplication; $(5 \bullet (3 + (4 + 7))) \bullet 9$ using the associative property of addition.
4. $(78{,}923{,}234 \bullet 2) \bullet 5 = 78{,}923{,}234 \bullet (2 \bullet 5) = 78{,}923{,}234 \bullet 10 = 789{,}232{,}340$
5. $\frac{3}{5} + (-\frac{3}{5} + \frac{12}{19}) = (\frac{3}{5} + -\frac{3}{5}) + \frac{12}{19} = 0 + \frac{12}{19} = \frac{12}{19}$

Chapter 4: Practice: Distributive Properties (p. 31–32)

1. 93
2. 8
3. Yes
4. $(3 \bullet 15) + (3 \bullet 5) = 3 \bullet (15 + 5) = 3 \bullet 20 = 60$.
5. $32a + 18a = (32 + 18)a = 50a$; $(16 + 9)2a$
6. Yes
7. 72
8. $(981 \bullet 53) + (19 \bullet 53) = (981 + 19) \bullet 53 = 1{,}000 \bullet 53 = 53{,}000$
9. $(819 \bullet 50) - (19 \bullet 50) = (819 - 19) \bullet 50 = 800 \bullet 50 = 40{,}000$
10. $3b + 4c$
11. $30 \bullet (20 + 4) = (30 \bullet 20) + (30 \bullet 4)$. This can be computed as $600 + 120 = 720$.
12. $(\frac{1}{5} \bullet 31) + (\frac{1}{5} \bullet 14) = \frac{1}{5} \bullet (31 + 14) = \frac{1}{5}(45) = 9$.
13. $9a + 12b = 3 \bullet (3a + 4b)$. One has to see that 3 is a factor of both 9 and 12.
14. $43a^5 + 9a^2 = (43a^3 + 9)a^2 = a^2 \bullet (43a^3 + 9)$
15. $-8z^2 + 4z = -4z(2z - 1)$ or $-8z^2 + 4z = 4z(-2z + 1)$

Chapter 4: Challenge Problems: Distributive Properties (p. 32)

1. $42 \bullet (\frac{3}{7} + \frac{5}{21}) = 42 \bullet \frac{3}{7} + 42 \bullet \frac{5}{21} = 6 \bullet 3 + 2 \bullet 5 = 18 + 10 = 28$
2. Yes, this statement is always true. It is also true that $(b - c) \bullet a = (b \bullet a) - (b \bullet c)$. If you have not already done so, try several examples to convince yourself that this is true.
   Let $a = 5$, $b = 9$, and $c = 2$. Let $a = 10$, $b = 8$, and $c = 11$.
3. There are several possible answers.
   One way is to think $48 \bullet 12 = (50 - 2) \bullet 12 = (50 \bullet 12) - (2 \bullet 12) = 600 - 24 = 576$.
   Another way is to think $48 \bullet 12 = (40 + 8) \bullet 12 = (40 \bullet 12) + (8 \bullet 12) = 480 + 96 = 576$.
   A third way to think is $48 \bullet 12 = 48 \bullet (10 + 2) = (48 \bullet 10) + (48 \bullet 2) = 480 + 96 = 576$.

Practice Answer Keys (cont.)

4. $\frac{5}{17} \cdot (34 + 85) = (\frac{5}{17} \cdot 34) + (\frac{5}{17} \cdot 85) = (5 \cdot 2) + (5 \cdot 5) = 10 + 25 = 35$

5. There are numerous solutions. One solution is $(3 + 7) \cdot 4 = (3 \cdot 4) + (7 \cdot 4)$.

6. $\frac{3}{7} \cdot (\frac{14}{3} + \frac{28}{9}) = (\frac{3}{7} \cdot \frac{14}{3}) + (\frac{3}{7} \cdot \frac{28}{9}) = \frac{2}{1} + \frac{4}{3} = \frac{10}{3}$.

Chapter 4: Part 1: Checking Progress All Properties (p. 33–34)

1. Identity Property of Addition

2. Commutative Property of Multiplication

3. Multiplicative Inverse Property

4. Distributive Property of Multiplication over Addition

5. Distributive Property of Multiplication over Subtraction

6. Associative Property of Addition

7. Commutative Property of Addition

8. Identity Property of Multiplication

9. Identity Property of Multiplication

10. Distributive Property of Multiplication over Addition

11. Identity Property of Addition

12. Additive Identity Property

13. Commutative Property of Addition

14. Distributive Property of Multiplication over Subtraction

15. Additive Inverse Property

16. Associative Property of Addition

17. Commutative Property of Multiplication

18. Identity Property of Multiplication

19. Distributive Property of Multiplication over Addition

20. Distributive Property of Multiplication over Subtraction

Practice Answer Keys (cont.)

Chapter 5: Practice: Exponential Expressions (p. 36–37)

1. 216
2. 25
3. 1,000,000,000,000,000
4. 729
5. -64
6. 0.027
7. 0.000027
8. $\frac{1}{25}$
9. 225
10. 2.25
11. 225,000
12. -225
13. 225
14. 729
15. 216
16. 38,416
17. 268,435,456
18. -6,436,343
19. These have the same value, -6,436,343.
20. $\frac{25}{9}$
21. 335.54432
22. 14,641
23. 12,321
24. 12,345,654,321
25. $9^2 = 81$; $99^2 = 9,801$; $999^2 = 998,001$; $9999^2 = 99,980,001$.
    Did you correctly predict $999,999^2 = 999,998,000,001$?

Chapter 5: Challenge Problems: Exponential Expressions (p. 37)

1. Ali is correct. Remember that by order of operations, exponentiation is completed first. Barb was providing a correct answer for a different expression, $(-5)^2$.
2. Be Careful. If $y = 0$, y^0 is undefined. For all other real number values for y, $y^0 = 1$.
3. This can be written in several ways. The most common ones you would see are $64 = 64^1$; $64 = 8^2$; $64 = 4^3$; and $64 = 2^6$.
4. Noah is right sometimes, but not always. For example, he is right with the expressions $2^6 = 64$ and $2^3 = 8$, but he is not right with $2^6 = 64$ and $4^3 = 64$.
5. If $a = b$, $a \neq 0$, and $b \neq 0$, this is true. If $a = 4$ and $b = 2$, it is true, as $2^4 = 4^2 = 16$.
6. 7, because $3^7 = 2,187$ and $3^8 = 6,561$

Practice Answer Keys (cont.)

Chapter 5: Practice: Exponential Expressions With Coefficients (p. 38–39)

1. 45
2. -75
3. $100b$
4. 810
5. 900
6. -1,215
7. -9,375
8. $100b^3$
9. $-1,681b^{41}$
10. $900a^{12}$
11. 108
12. 1,728
13. 1,728
14. -1,728
15. 900
16. 32,400
17. 3,600
18. 8,100
19. 700,000
20. 1,000,000

Chapter 5: Challenge Problems: Exponential Expressions With Coefficients (p. 39)

1. Disagree. The computation should be, $3^2 = 9$; $5 \bullet 9 = 45$.
2. Yes, they do give the same value.
3. 89,450
4. 0.00162
5. 0.23152

Chapter 5: Practice: Addition and Subtraction of Exponential Expressions With Like Terms (p. 40–41)

1. $23z^3$
2. $9(320) = 2,880$
3. $-8z^3$
4. $-12(2^3) = -96$
5. $-30z^2$
6. $7a^4$
7. $19a^4$
8. $5^4(9^2 + 2^3) = 5^4(81 + 8) = 5^4(89) = 55,625$
9. $5^4(a^2 + a^3)$. Other variations include $625(a^2 + a^3)$; or $5^4a^2(1 + a)$; or $625a^2(1 + a)$.
10. $25a^2 - b^4$

Practice Answer Keys (cont.)

11. $25a^2 + 67b^4$
12. $2s^4 + 2s^3$
13. $2s^3$
14. 0
15. $-34n^2$
16. $6(a^{15} + b^{15} + c^{15})$; or $6a^{15} + 6b^{15} + 6c^{15}$
17. This is the same as the previous problem.
18. This could be considered as simplified.
    Another way to write it would be $a^{13}(a^2 + 2a + 3) + b^{13}(b^2 + 2b + 3) + c^{13}(c^2 + 2c + 3)$.
19. $(2^3 + 3^3 + 4^3 + 5^3)a^7 = 224a^7$
20. $7 \cdot 7^5$. This is usually written as $7^6 = 117,649$
21. $373 \cdot 7^5 = 6,269,011$
22. $-402,830,176$
23. No. $18^3 - 18^2 = 5,508$
24. 34^7
25. 1, 2, 3, 4, and 5.

Chapter 5: Challenge Problems: Addition and Subtraction With Like Terms (p. 41)

1. Disagree. About the only way to rewrite it would be to use the distributive property and write it as, $z \cdot (3z + 5)$.
2. No! $1^2 + 2^2 + 3^2 = 1 + 4 + 9 = 13$; $(1 + 2 + 3)^2 = 6^2 = 36$
3. $(38w^8 - 13z^5)$
4. $b^2 - 6a - c^{15} + c$
5. 1 and 2
6. Disagree. Macy's solution would be $14^5 = 537,824$, which is not correct. The correct answer is $-402,830,176$.

Chapter 5: Practice: Multiplication and Division of Exponential Expressions (p. 43)

1. p^8
2. 3^{11}
3. 3^2
4. x^2
5. 15^2
6. $2x^2$
7. 4^{18}
8. 5^4
9. 1
10. 5^6
11. 11^4
12. 13^{42}
13. $a^{13}b^{59}$
14. a^5b^{45}

Practice Answer Keys (cont.)

15. $\dfrac{a^5}{b^{27}} = a^5 \div b^{27}$

16. $a^{13}b^{27}$

17. $\dfrac{a^5}{b^{45}} = a^5 \div b^{45}$

18. $s^{38}t^{28}$
19. $(19^7 \bullet 3^{16})$
20. $3^{18} \bullet 5^7$

Chapter 5: Challenge Problems: Multiplication and Division of Exponential Expressions (p. 44)

1. Yes, these have the same value. Another way to write either is 3^8.
2. Disagree. $13^5 \bullet 13^7 = 13^{12}$, while $(13^5)^7 = 13^{35}$.

3. Disagree. $\dfrac{11^{42}}{11^{21}} = 11^{(42-21)} = 11^{21}$

4. Disagree. $\dfrac{11^{42}}{11^{-42}} = 11^{(42-(-42))} = 11^{84}$

5. s is an integer greater than 4. That is, s is an element of the set {5, 6, 7, 8, …}.

Chapter 5: Practice: Raising to a Power, Including Negative Exponents (p. 46)

1. 3^{12}
2. 7^0 or 1
3. 2^9
4. x^{10}

5. $\dfrac{1}{5^4} = \dfrac{1}{625} = 0.0016$

6. $\dfrac{1}{2^5} = \dfrac{1}{32} = 0.03125$

7. 7^{30}
8. These have the same value.

9. $\dfrac{1}{5^2} = \dfrac{1}{25} = 0.04$

10. 61^6

11. They are not the same. $(-13)^2 = 169$ and $13^{-2} = \dfrac{1}{169}$.

Practice Answer Keys (cont.)

12. $\left(\dfrac{43^2}{13^3}\right)$

13. 1
14. 1
15. 1

16. $\dfrac{-1}{2^5} = \dfrac{-1}{32} = -0.03125$

17. $\dfrac{-1}{2^8} = \dfrac{-1}{256} = -0.00390625$

18. $(-2)^7 = -128$
19. y^{150}
20. 2^{150}

Chapter 5: Challenge Problems Raising to a Power, Including Negative Exponents (p. 47)

1. $\left(\frac{1}{5}\right)^{-3}$ is larger. $\left(\frac{1}{5}\right)^{-3} = (5^{-1})^{-3} = 5^3 = 125$; $5^2 = 25$

2. Makenzie is correct.

3. Emil is correct. $\left(-\frac{1}{4}\right)^{-3} = \left(-4^{-1}\right)^{-3} = \left(-4\right)^3 = -64$

4. Disagree. The value is $7^{-9} = \dfrac{1}{7^9} = \dfrac{1}{40{,}353{,}607}$.

5. $x = 7$

Chapter 5: Practice: Scientific Notation (p. 48–49)

1. 4,324,000,000
2. 12,312,324; $1.2312324 \cdot 10^7$
3. $3.404 \cdot 10^{-3}$
4. $0.0034561 \cdot 10^2$
5. $4.39923 \cdot 10^3$
6. $5{,}784 \cdot 2{,}200 = 12{,}724{,}800 = 1.27248 \cdot 10^7$
7. $5.784 \cdot 2.2 = 12.7248 = 1.27248 \cdot 10$
8. $(5.784 \cdot 10^5) \cdot (2.2 \cdot 10^{-8}) = 12.7248 \cdot 10^{-3} = 1.27248 \cdot 10^{-2}$
9. $t = 4$
10. $t = -5$
11. 0.0012312324; $1.2312324 \cdot 10^{-3}$
12. 482,992; $4.82992 \cdot 10^5$
13. $4.032 \cdot 10^4$
14. $z = 518.40$
15. $z = 14$

Practice Answer Keys (cont.)

Chapter 5: Challenge Problems: Scientific Notation (p. 49)

1. $\frac{1}{256} = 0.00390625 = 3.90625 \cdot 10^{-3}$

2. $\frac{5}{16} = 0.3125 = 3.125 \cdot 10^{-1}$

3. $\frac{0.09}{200} = 0.00045 = 4.5 \cdot 10^{-4}$

4. $\frac{(222.5)(10^5)}{(4)(10^2)} = 55.625 \cdot 10^3 = 5.5625 \cdot 10^4$

5. $\frac{(222.5)(10^2)}{(0.04)(10^5)} = 5562.5 \cdot 10^{-3} = 5.5625 \cdot 10^0$

Chapter 5: Checking Progress: Exponents and Exponential Expressions (p. 50)

1. 0.0000000032
2. -64
3. 15
4. 640
5. 216
6. $25a^2 - 67b^4$
7. $59a^2 - 67b^4$
8. $a^{55} \cdot b^{100}$

9. $\frac{1}{2^4}$; $\frac{1}{16} = 0.0625$

10. y^{100}
11. $1.278264 \cdot 10^2$
12. $t = -4$

Chapter 6: Practice: Square Roots (p. 54–56)

1. 7
2. 9
3. 10
4. 50
5. 0.6
6. $10\sqrt{3}$
7. 20
8. $0.2 = \frac{2}{10} = \frac{1}{5}$
9. $2\sqrt{10}$
10. 11
11. $11\sqrt{10}$
12. 1

13. 125
14. $25\sqrt{3}$
15. 12
16. 60
17. 30
18. 280
19. 280
20. 312
21. $4z$
22. $4z^2$
23. $4z^3$
24. $4z^6\sqrt{z}$

25. $9y^{11}$
26. x^2y
27. $8x^3y^2z^4$
28. $672x^3y^2z^4$
29. z
30. z^5
31. x^2z^4
32. $x^2z^3\sqrt{xz}$
33. xyz
34. xyz
35. xy
36. $126\sqrt{6}$

37. $3\sqrt{2}$
38. $2\sqrt{15}$
39. 30
40. $30\sqrt{6}$
41. $7\sqrt{6}$
42. $3\sqrt{2}$
43. 70
44. $5\sqrt{14}$
45. $140\sqrt{3}$
46. $3\sqrt{5}$
47. $3\sqrt{3}$
48. $2\sqrt{2}$

Practice Answer Keys (cont.)

49. $5\sqrt{5}$
50. $2\sqrt{7}$
51. $7^2\sqrt{7} = 49\sqrt{7}$
52. $7\sqrt{2}$
53. $4\sqrt{3}$
54. $3\sqrt{5}$
55. $5^4\sqrt{5} = 625\sqrt{5}$
56. $\frac{6}{5}$ or 1.2
57. $\frac{9}{4}$ or 2.25
58. $\frac{4}{3}\sqrt{3}$ or $\frac{4\sqrt{3}}{3}$

59. $\frac{35}{32}$ or 1.09375

60. $\frac{7}{4}\sqrt{2}$ or $\frac{7\sqrt{2}}{4}$ or equivalent

61. $\frac{1}{2}\sqrt{10}$ or $\frac{\sqrt{10}}{2}$ or equivalent

62. $\frac{1}{5}\sqrt{3}$ or equivalent
63. $\frac{5}{3}\sqrt{5}$ or equivalent
64. $\frac{6}{7}\sqrt{7}$ or equivalent
65. $\frac{5}{7}$
66. $\frac{1}{3}\sqrt{5}$
67. $\frac{4}{5}\sqrt{15}$
68. $\frac{1}{6}\sqrt{30}$
69. $\frac{2}{15}\sqrt{55}$
70. $\frac{4}{25}\sqrt{330}$

Chapter 6: Challenge Problems: Simplifying Each Expression (p. 56–57)

1. $3\sqrt{2}$
2. While these two expression look different, they both have the value of $\frac{7}{10} = 0.7$.
3. 0.1 or $\frac{1}{10}$
4. $(0.1)(0.3) = 0.03$
5. $0.049\sqrt{70}$

Chapter 6: Practice: Adding and Subtracting Radicals (p. 57–58)

1. 23
2. $11\sqrt{x}$
3. Cannot be simplified
4. $14\sqrt{5}$
5. $-22\sqrt{2y}$
6. $5\sqrt{2y}$
7. $2y\sqrt{3y} + \sqrt{3y} = (2y + 1)\sqrt{3y}$
8. 0
9. $-6y^2\sqrt{6}$
10. $4y^2\sqrt{6}$
11. $3\sqrt{6} + (y - 1)\sqrt{6y}$
12. $9\sqrt{5}$
13. 13
14. 169
15. No values. $\sqrt{3y} + 9\sqrt{3y} = 10\sqrt{3y}$ for $y > 0$

Chapter 6: Challenge Problems: Adding and Subtracting Radicals (p. 58)

1. Disagree. These are not equivalent expressions.
2. $5\sqrt{7}$
3. Agree. Jill is correct.
4. Disagree. $5\sqrt{3} + 5\sqrt{3} = 10\sqrt{3}$
5. $y > 4$ (or $y \geq 5$)

Practice Answer Keys (cont.)

Chapter 6: Checking Progress: Square Roots and Radicals (p. 59)

1. 35
2. 33
3. $13z^7$
4. $a^3z^7\sqrt{az}$
5. $2^2 \cdot 7^2 \cdot 23\sqrt{46}$
6. 28
7. $\dfrac{2\sqrt{26}}{13}$
8. 1
9. $16\sqrt{3z}$
10. $-2\sqrt{5z}$

Chapter 7: Practice: Generalizing Patterns in Number Lists and Tables (p. 61)

1. A) 16, 22, 29
   B) "Start by adding 1 to the first term and add one more each time." That is, $1 + 1 = 2$, $2 + 2 = 4$, $4 + 3 = 7$, $7 + 4 = 11$, etc.
2. A) 20, 26, 33
   B) Note, this is the same pattern as in problem 1 except the first number is 5 not 1. The 15th term is 110.
3. A) 1, 2, 1
   B) The 200th term is 2.
   C) The 1,000th term is 2.
4. -49
5. $3 \cdot 55 = 165$
6. A) 55th term is 109. $2 \cdot (55) - 1$
   B) 98th term is $55 \cdot 49 = 2,695$.
7. -70
8. First term is $3 + 2(1) = 5$. Second term is $3 + 2(2) = 7$. Similarly, the next terms are 9, 11, 13, 15.
9. 4, 1, 0, 1, 4, 9, 16, 25, 36, 49
10. Yes, the 5th term in each sequence will be 44.

Chapter 7: Challenge Problems: Patterns in Number Lists (p. 62)

1. A) 25, 36, 49;
   B) The 30th term is $30^2 = 900$.
2. A) 16, 19, 22;
   B) The 200th term is 598.
3. A) 22, 25, 28;
   B) The 200th term is 607. [Can you see any relationship to Challenge Problem 2?]

Practice Answer Keys (cont.)

4. $431^2 = 185,761$
5. 1,211

Chapter 7: Challenge Problems: Patterns in Tables (p. 62–66)

1. A) 23
   B) 19
   C) "add two to the input to obtain the output"
   D) If n is input, output is $n + 2$.
2. A) -9
   B) 11
   C) "double the input and add one to obtain the output"
   D) If n is the input, output is $2n + 1$.
3. A) 30
   B) 16
   C) output is $80 - 5n$
4. A) 61
   B) 78
   C) 5 and -5 as inputs give 22 as an output
5. A) -12
   B) 44
   C) "subtract 1 from the input and double it to obtain the output"
   D) If n is the input, output is $2(n - 1)$.
6. A) 14
   B) 25
   C) "subtract 1 from input, double the result, subtract this result from 52"
   D) If n is the input, output is $52 - 2(n - 1)$. [This is equivalent to $54 - 2n$, which would be written in words, "double the input and subtract it from 54."]
   E) 60
7. A) 89
   B) 104
   C) "subtract 1 from the input, multiply the result by four and add the result to 13";
   D) If n is the input, output is $13 + 4(n - 1)$. [This is equivalent to $4n + 9$, which would be written in words, multiply the input by 4 and add 9.]
   E) -3
8. A) 73
   B) 5
   C) If n is the input, output is $8n - 7$.
9. A) 89
   B) 6
   C) If n is the input, output is $(n + 3) \cdot 7 - 2$.

Practice Answer Keys (cont.)

10. A) 90
    B) 8 or -6
    C) If n is the input, output is $(n - 1)^2 + 9$.

Chapter 7: Challenge Problems: Generalizing Patterns in Tables (p. 66–67)

1. A) -7
   B) 10
   C) "double the input plus 3 gives the output"
   D) If n is the input, output is $2n + 3$.
2. A) For the input of -5, the output is -9.
   B) For the output of 23, the input is 3.
   C) The rule in symbols: $3(x + 2) + (x + 5)$

Input	Output
1	15
5	31
-2	3
-4	-5
0	11

3. A) 4
   B) 6 or -12
   C) "add 3 to the input and square the result"
   D) If n is the input, output is $(n + 3)^2$.
4. A) For the input of -5, the output is 42.
   B) For the output of 30, the input is 7 or -4.
   C) The rule in symbols is $(x - 1)^2 + 1 - x$.

Input	Output
1	0
5	12
-2	12
-4	30
0	2

Practice Answer Keys (cont.)

Chapter 7: Practice: Generalizing Patterns in Algebraic Expressions and Equations (p. 68–69)

1. $x^2 - 7$; EXP
2. $3x + 6$; EXP
3. $2x + 7 = 15$; EQ
4. $2x + 10$; EXP
5. $\frac{1}{2}x - 12 = 8$; EQ
6. $18 + 12x = 50$; EQ
7. $7x + 10$; EXP
8. $15 = \frac{1}{2}(x + 8) - 40$; EQ
9. $2x - \frac{1}{3}x$; EXP
10. $2(x + 10)$; EXP
11. $x + (x + 1) + (x + 2) + (x + 3) + (x + 4) + (x + 5) + (x + 6)$; EXP
12. $\frac{1}{2}x - 8 = 40$; EQ
13. $x + 40 = \frac{1}{2}x + 60$; EQ
14. $x + 6 + 12 + 18 = 120$; EQ
15. $x - 10 + 3x = 80$; EQ

Chapter 7: Challenge Problems: Generalizing Patterns in Algebraic Expressions and Equations (p. 69)

1. $x + 50 = 10 - x$; EQ
2. $2x - \frac{1}{3}x = x - 9$; EQ
3. $2(x + 10) = 3x - 5$; EQ
4. $x + (x + 1) + (x + 2) + (x + 3) + (x + 4) + (x + 5) + (x + 6) = 5(x + 6)$; EQ

Chapter 7: Part 1: Practice: Using Algebra to Generalize Patterns Solving Simple Linear Equations (p. 71)

1. $x = -6$
2. $a = 29$
3. $x = 7$
4. $x = -18$
5. $b = 7$
6. $x = -7$
7. $a = 32$
8. $x = 11$
9. $x = -9$
10. $b = \frac{16}{7}$

Practice Answer Keys (cont.)

Chapter 7: Challenge Problems: Using Algebra to Generalize Patterns Solving Linear Equations (p. 71)

1. No value of *x* will work.
2. $a = 3$
3. $x = 5$
4. $x = -\frac{10}{6}$
5. $x = \frac{57}{13}$

Chapter 7: Part 2: Practice: Using Algebra to Generalize Patterns Solving Linear Equations (p. 72)

1. $x = -14$
2. $m = 17$
3. $x = -1$
4. $x = 5$
5. $b = 6$
6. $x = 9$
7. $x = 6$
8. $x = -\frac{9}{4} = -2.25$
9. $x = 2$
10. $x = -8.3$
11. $x = -1.5$
12. $x = 2$
13. $x = 5$
14. $x = 15$
15. $x = \frac{11}{12}$
16. $x = 0.01$
17. $x = 100$
18. $x = \frac{56}{3}$
19. $x = \frac{-2}{13}$
20. $x = 0$

Chapter 7: Checking Progress: Using Algebra to Generalize Patterns Numbers (p. 73–74)

1. A) 47, 53, 59;
   B) 15th term is 101
2. -96
3. The 6th term in each will be 35.

Practice Answer Keys (cont.)

4. A) -24
   B) 9
   C) "multiply input by 5 and add 1"
   D) If input is n, $5n + 1$ is output.
5. A) 7
   B) -4

   C) If n is input, $(n + 2) - \frac{1}{2}n$, is the output.

   D) The expression $(n + 2) - \frac{1}{2}n$ is equivalent to $\frac{1}{2}n + 2$.
6. A) 35
   B) 48
   C) "subtract one from the input, double it, and add it to -3"
   D) If n is the input, $-3 + 2(n - 1)$ is the output. The expression $-3 + 2(n - 1)$ is equivalent to $2n - 5$.
   E) -11
7. $2(n + 7) = 15$

8. $n - (\frac{1}{2}n + 1)$
9. $a = 3$
10. $x = -6$

Chapter 8: Practice: Problem Solving With Tables (p. 76–77)
1. Dan has $35, Chris has $45.
2. Sports drink = 100 bottles, cola = 200 bottles, water = 300 bottles.
3. 4,096 bacteria
4. 169 m^2
5. At 16 months
6. 80
7. 72
8. $16
9. 4
10. 91

Chapter 8: Practice: Using Linear Equations to Solve Problems (p. 80–81)
1. $B + (B + 0.5) = 24$; One board is 11.75′, and the other is 12.25′.
2. $L + \frac{1}{4}L = 60$; Lei has 48 books, and Tyrone has 12 books.
3. $N + (6 + N) = 12$; 9 jurors voted to convict.
4. $K + (K - 16) = 40$; Laticia had 12 pencils, and Kim had 28 pencils.
5. $S + (S + 20) = 400$; Sivart wrote190 questions, and Brab wrote 210 questions.
6. $S + (3S - 5) = 79$; Skyler made 21 visits, and Elaine made 58 visits.
7. $3L + 2 = 86$; 28

Practice Answer Keys (cont.)

8. $n \div 2 = 3n - 15$; 6
9. $0.34x + 0.27(20 - x) = 6.45$; 15 $0.34 stamps and 5 $0.27 stamps
10. $5(L + 11) + 6L = 495$; Small bus, 40; larger bus, 51.

Chapter 8: Challenge Problems: Problem Solving (p. 81–82)

1. $B + (12.25 \bullet 10) = 137.50$; $15
2. $78 + 0.40(m - 550) = 98$; 50 minutes
3. Make a table to solve the problem: 400 bottles and no paper; 398 bottles and 5 pounds of paper; 396 bottles and 10 pounds of paper, … no bottles and 1,000 pounds of paper.
4. $\dfrac{4}{3} = \dfrac{4,520}{L}$; 7,910 votes
5. $B + 1.75(6) = 17.45$; $6.95
6. $12S + 2(2S + 8) = 112$; Tie, $20; scarf, $6

Chapter 8: Checking Progress: Problem-Solving Strategies (p. 82–83)

1. Total cost is: $f + 37.50h = 97.50$; $20 flat rate.
2. $S + (S - 30) = 400$; Selena wrote 215 questions, and Peyton wrote 185 questions.
3. $\frac{1}{2}g + ((11 \bullet 2) - 9) = g - 2(14)$; 82 years old
4. $4V + 3V = 4,550$; 2,600 votes
5. $5.55 + 6t = 13.95$; $1.40 per topping
6. $P + (2P + 12) = 873$; Pizza – 287; Ice Cream – 586
7. $4s - 9 = 3s + 82$; 91
8. $8L + 2(\frac{1}{2}L + 8) = 556$; Large bus, 60; small bus, 38

Check-Up Answer Keys

Check-Up Problems: Real Numbers (p. 84)
1. Real Number, Rational Number
2. Whole Number, Integer, Rational Number, Real Number
3. Irrational Number, Real Number
4. Real Number, Rational Number
5. Real Number, Rational Number
6. Integer, Real Number, Whole Number, Rational Number
7. Real Number, Rational Number
8. Rational Number, Real Number
9. Real Number, Irrational Number
10. None of the above

Check-Up Problems: Operations of Numbers and Variables (p. 85)
1. $123s$
2. 5.493
3. $\frac{13}{15}$
4. $\frac{2}{5}$
5. $4.32345ab$
6. $0.08ab = \frac{2}{25}ab$
7. $\frac{9}{10}$
8. $\frac{xz}{20}$
9. 6
10. -28.8

Check-Up Problems: Integers (p. 86)
1. 2
2. 16
3. 10
4. -338
5. 49,544
6. 0
7. -3
8. 18
9. 11
10. -80

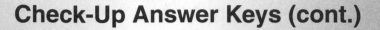

Check-Up Answer Keys (cont.)

Check-Up Problems: Properties (p. 87)

1. -62
2. 122
3. $219b$
4. $(290z + 413a)$
5. 1,287
6. $(923,234 \cdot 2) \cdot 5 = 923,234 \cdot (2 \cdot 5) = 923,234 \cdot 10 = 9,232,340$
7. $(13 \cdot 15) + (13 \cdot 5) = 13 \cdot (15 + 5) = 13 \cdot 20 = 260$
8. $(31b + 14c)$
9. $b^5(43b^3 + 19)$
10. Commutative property of addition.

Check-Up Problems: Exponents and Exponential Expressions (p. 88)

1. 0.000027
2. -125
3. 6
4. 14,400
5. 216
6. $21a^2 - 67b^4$
7. $21a^2 + b^4$
8. $a^{45} \cdot b^{27}$

9. $\dfrac{1}{3^3}$; $\dfrac{1}{27}$

10. y^{120}
11. $1.02696 \cdot 10^3$
12. 3

Check-Up Problems: Square Roots (p. 89)

1. 54
2. 29
3. $11z^6$
4. $a^5 z^{12}\sqrt{z}$
5. $2^4 \cdot 11^2 \cdot 13\sqrt{22}$
6. $12\sqrt{5}$

7. $\dfrac{\sqrt{55}}{5}$

8. $\sqrt{3}$
9. $(z - 4)\sqrt{2z}$
10. $(3z^2 + 10z)\sqrt{6z}$, or $z(3z + 10)\sqrt{6z}$

Check-Up Answer Keys (cont.)

Check-Up Problems: Using Algebra to Generalize Patterns (p. 90–91)

1. 15, 19, 23; 51
2. 1,233
3. The 6th term in each sequence is 38.
4. A) -12
   B) 40
   C) "add one to the input, and multiply by three" or "multiply the input by 3, and then add 3"
   D) If n is the input, $3(n + 1)$ or $3n + 3$ is the output.
5. A) 19
   B) -28
   C) If n is the input, $\frac{1}{2}n + 14$ is the output.
6. A) -33
   B) 17
   C) "triple the input and subtract result from 27"
   D) If n is input, $27 - 3n$ is output.
   E) 36
7. $42 - 2(n + 8) = 16$
8. $3(n + 9) - 6$
9. $b = 7$
10. $x = 1.5$

Check-Up Problems: Problem-Solving Strategies (92–93)

1. $2w + 2(w + 24) = 120$; Length is 42 yards and width is 18 yards.
2. Total cost: $6s + 8.95$; $25
3. $2(w + 3) + 2(2w + 3) = 186$; width is 32' and, and length is 61'
4. $\frac{4}{3} = \frac{W}{L}$; $\frac{4}{3} = \frac{W}{4,521}$; $W = 6,028$; $L + W = 10,549$ votes
5. x = time: $11x + 14x = 100$; $x = 4$; $11(4) = 44$ miles
6. $14 + \frac{1}{3}m = (14 - 11) + 1 + \frac{1}{2}m$; 60 years
7. $B + 6(1.35) = 13.45$; $5.35
8. $H + (\frac{1}{3}H + 13) = 397$; Haunted House = 288; Twister = 109.
9. $5s - 9 = 4s + 82$; 91
10. $9S + 3(2S + 5) = 255$; Large bus, 37; small bus, 16

References

References

Brown, R., Dolciani, M., Sorgenfrey, R., Cole, W., (1997). *Algebra structure and method book 1.* Evanston, IL: McDougal Littell.

Chicago Mathematics Project (found online July 2004). *Connected mathematics.* University of Chicago. Found online at: http://www.math.msu.edu/cmp/curriculum/Algebra.htm

Edwards, E. (1990). *Algebra for everyone.* Reston, VA: National Council of Teachers of Mathematics.

Long, L. (1998). *Painless algebra.* Hauppauge, NY: Barron's Educational Series.

National Council of Teachers of Mathematics (NCTM). (2000). *Principles and standards for school mathematics.* Reston, VA: National Council of Teachers of Mathematics.

National Council of Teachers of Mathematics (NCTM). (2004). *Standards and expectations for algebra.* Reston, VA: National Council of Teachers of Mathematics. Found online at: http://www.nctm.org

Freudenthal Institute at the University of Utrecht / University of Wisconsin / NSF (found online July 2004) *Math in context.* http://www.showmecenter.missouri.edu/showme/mic.shtml Encyclopedia Britannica.

Web Resources

Algebra.help. (2001–2004)
http://www.algebrahelp.com/index.jsp

Algebra Solutions
http://www.gomath.com/algebra.html

Awesome Library—Algebra
http://www.awesomelibrary.org/Classroom/Mathematics/Middle-High_School_Math/Algebra.html

Borenson, H. (2001–2004) *Hands on Equations.* Allentown, PA: Borenson and Associates. Found online at: http://www.borenson.com/?src=overture

Brennon, J. (2002) *Understanding algebra.* Found online at: http://www.jamesbrennan.org/algebra/

References (cont.)

Common Core State Standards Initiative—Mathematics
http://www.corestandards.org/Math

Cool Math Sites
http://www.cte.jhu.edu/techacademy/web/2000/heal/mathsites.htm

Ed Helper.com
http://www.edhelper.com/algebra.htm

History of Algebra
http://www.ucs.louisiana.edu/~sxw8045/history.htm

Holt, Rinehart, and Winston Mathematics in Context
http://www.hrw.com/math/mathincontext/index.htm

Interactive Mathematic Miscellany and Puzzles
http://www.cut-the-knot.org/algebra.shtml

Introduction to Algebra
http://www.mathleague.com/help/algebra/algebra.htm

Math Archives: Topics in Mathematics, Algebra
http://www.archives.math.utk.edu/topics/algebra.html

Moses, B. *The algebra project.* Cambridge, MA: The Algebra Project, Inc.
http://www.algebra.org/index.html

Oracle Education Foundation Think Quest Library (2004) Algebra
Found online at: http://library.thinkquest.org/10030/algecon.htm

Reichman, H. and Kohn, M. (2004) *Math made easy.*
Found online at: http://mathmadeeasy.com/algebra.html

Reliable problem solving in all subjects that use mathematics for problem solving. Algebra, Physics, Chemistry... from grade school to grad school and beyond.
http://www2.hawaii.edu/suremath/intro_algebra.html

Show Me Center
http://www.showmecenter.missouri.edu/showme/

SOS Mathematics
http://www.sosmath.com/

References (cont.)

Surfing the Net With Kids
http://www.surfnetkids.com/algebra.htm

The Math Forum Drexel University (1994–2004) K–12 Internet Algebra Resources. Philadelphia, PA.
http://mathforum.org/algebra/k12.algebra.html

University of Akron Theoretical and Applied Mathematics
http://www.math.uakron.edu/~dpstory/mpt_home.html

Real Life Applications of Math

Applied Academics: Applications of Mathematics—Careers
http://www.bced.gov.bc.ca/careers/aa/lessons/math.htm

Exactly How is Math Used in Technology?
http://www.math.bcit.ca/examples/index.shtml

Mathematics Association of America—Careers
http://www.maa.org/careers/index.html

NASA Space Link
http://www.spacelink.msfc.nasa.gov/.index.html